mad
bad
love

(and how the things we love can nearly kill us)

SARA-JAYNE MAKWALA KING

mf

Melinda Ferguson Books,
an imprint of NB Publishers, a division of Media24 Boeke (Pty) Ltd
40 Heerengracht, Cape Town, South Africa
PO Box 879, Cape Town 8000, South Africa
www.nb.co.za

Cover design and typography: Wilna Combrinck
Editor: Sean Fraser
Proofreader: Riaan Wolmarans
Set in Sabon LT Pro
Printed and bound by CTP Printers, Cape Town

First published by Melinda Ferguson Books 2022
First edition, first impression

ISBN: 978-1-990973-56-7
ISBN: 978-1-990973-57-4 (epub)

For the loves of my life – even the ones who nearly killed me

"If you heal, not only do you heal yourself, you heal all the women who came before you and you heal all the kin that is to come from you."
– Claire Phillips, South African singer-songwriter

Contents

Prologue

Confessions of a mad, bad mother

01:11am The Clinic – May 2019

I am a bad mother. I've always known I would be. I come from a place that insists that I could never have been anything else. The apple doesn't fall far from the tree. A scorpion is a scorpion is a scorpion. Here I am, not yet swollen with the anticipation of what's to come, and I have *already* failed at motherhood. I have failed and the guilt of it gnaws away at the same place in which I must nurture new life.

You cannot heal in the place you got sick – and yet this is the place I've come back to again and again. A place of healing *and* of sickness. The place where I met *him*. The one who, once upon another lifetime, seemed sent to save me from myself, and who, a few weeks ago, in the before of it all, delivered unto and into me what I've longed for all my life. But now he is gone, taken by his own demons, leaving me alone with a piece of his heart beating inside me.

Some people hate places like this. Places where there is a suggestion of dis-ease, a reminder of illness and of death. Perhaps that's exactly why I like it here and why I am no stranger to this place.

Every year I check myself into The Clinic. Every. Single. Year.

If I were "normal", I'd head to Plett or Knysna. Or maybe Thailand and lotus-pose the living shit out of myself, or perhaps I would float to Indonesia on a cloud of self-righteousness to rescue bull elephants from having bloated, sunburned tourists hitch a cultural lift on their thick-skinned, sturdy backs. I might even prostrate myself before wizened old babas in India in the hope that their eons of patiently perfected spirituality might somehow rub off on me through prayer, proximity or osmosis.

I retreat to The Clinic when the sound of my heart crashing against the inner wall of my chest is louder than the beat of my own drum. When "real life" has begun to interfere with the *life-on-life's-terms* type of life I've been trying to live since the first time I found myself here. Real life is the stuff that happens in between all those bullshit #lovinglife #lifegoals hashtags. It's what happens *after* you check in to your own arsehole on Facebook, or sanctimoniously post some dry witticism on Twitter, or send a plate of garlic-butter prawns into the Instagram ether just to let who-the-fuck-knows-or-cares *know* that you're #cleaneating again.

Real life is what happens between the "I'm fine", the "Thank you for coming" and the "For sure! See you next week". It squeezes itself into the small, guff-filled crevices left by the "we simply adored Paris last summer", the "Can't wait for First Thursdays!" and the "Look how fucking happy and in love and satisfied – sexually, spiritually and, of course, financially – we are and here's a picture to prove it". It deftly seizes the gap between "I'd love to" and "Just tell me when" and "Of course I don't mind *truly*" and it takes hold, burrowing its gnarled roots into the precarious, sandy foundation of this perilous adventure called life.

Real life does all of this and then, when it's properly anchored, takes an enormous, unceremonious dump on the false promise of make-believe. Given the opportunity, real life can, will and does jam its ugly, calloused, verruca-riddled foot into the door labelled *False Sense of Security* and kick you half to death. It's more than happy to leave you strewn across the bathroom floor, arms freshly diced and sliced by your own hand, gaping red and pissing self-hatred all over the Italian tiles. #Nofilter.

Real life is a leveller. Real life is sneaky as hell. Real life doesn't give a flying fuck.

One day I'd like to get to the point where the choice is maybe the Maldives or The Clinic. When the lull of the ocean has the same effect as 40 milligrams of Prozac, or when a walk on the beach at sunset provides a perfectly adequate alternative to Jungian therapy. "Holiday or hospital this year, SJ?" I'll muse while contemplating my half-packed suitcase and, before I'm even aware of what I'm doing, I'll fling a high-cut polka-dot two-piece into the case, kick the lid shut and that will be that. The ill-fitting bikini will seal the deal. But not this year. This year, because it's what I do, it's The Clinic.

Part I

1

You're nobody 'til somebody loves you

I was four years old the first time I fell in love. His name was Simon Shakespeare, he was eight and he went to school with my older brother, Adam. Simon was a white boy, unlike Adam. In fact, apart from Adam, I didn't know brown-boys like him existed, at least not in real life. There were, of course, the coloured-in brown boys I saw in storybooks, the ones with muddy, Crayola-brown skin, big pink lips, wide noses and skinny legs, but they weren't real. They were, for sure, the figment of some pasty illustrator's colonial imagination, but they didn't exist, not really. They were always barefoot, climbing trees and picking bananas. Like monkeys. Feral. They weren't like the peach-coloured boys in the adventure books in the library. Never were they in long pants, poring over treasure maps or pressing their eyes to the lenses of heavy binoculars while carrying backpacks stuffed with ham sandwiches and homemade lemonade. They weren't Famous Five material. The Aryan poster child I fell in love with, on the other hand, was iconic Enid Blyton. Buttery blond hair, alabaster skin and eyes that shone cornflower blue or pale agate, depending on how the sunlight reflected off them. I would see Simon every day when my mum and I would walk Adam to his school, the local primary a short distance from where we lived in a small pastoral village in Surrey in the south of England.

Before we'd even made it through the imposing wrought-iron gates into the school grounds to deliver Adam to his energetic classmates and weary-looking teacher, my love-hungry eyes would be scanning the playground. When I'd eventually clock my love interest, my entire stomach would drop into my heels and I would feel as if someone had poured warm, golden treacle into the spaces between my ribs. Even at four years old I knew what it felt like to fall in love, and I knew I liked it. Even at four years old I knew what it was to flirt, balancing myself on one foot like a miniature ballerina, twirling the hem of Mum's thick corduroy skirt in my fat little hands, grinning coquettishly up at an oblivious Simon. Even at four years old I knew I wanted him to love me back.

On the couple of mornings each week when Mum dropped me at the adjacent nursery school, I could pursue my infatuation from afar. The nursery's large bay windows overlooked the playground where Adam and Simon and the other children who went to Big School would be let out for playtime. When the bell rang, I would rush over to the window and press my nose up against the glass. From there I would watch my crush playing cops and robbers, shooting mortal enemies from the tips of his gun fingers or kicking a ball into the makeshift goal the boys had fashioned using a sweater and someone's lunchbox. I would watch him until the bell rang again, summoning him back inside to recite his times table.

Unsurprisingly, Simon had no interest in me, nor any idea that he was the object of my affections, and he barely acknowledged me beyond being his pal's annoying little sister. But that mattered little to me; I simply *pretended* that my affections were reciprocated. At the nursery, I would play "Mummies and Daddies" with the other boys and girls. It was one of my favourite make-believe games. I loved playing house. I loved imagining and creating my own family. We'd excitedly delve into the musty dress-up box and transform ourselves into short, badly dressed versions of our own parents. The girls clip-clopping around in too-big ladies' court shoes, tailored jackets with enormous shoulder pads and handbags and the boys pulling on police or firemen's helmets or taking turns to proudly lug around a battered leather briefcase with a broken clasp, presumably donated by one of the real-life Daddies. Once kitted out in our grown-up gear, the girls would pour imaginary tea into cups, sipping daintily, while the boys would inform us that they were "going out to work" and instruct us, in their squeaky little-boy voices, to "look after the baby". Each time we played, my vivid imagination cast Simon in the role as Daddy to my Mummy.

One day, when the classroom doors burst open and dozens of big little people spilled out onto the asphalt, I watched as first Simon and then a girl I recognised from my brother's class as Josephine Barker made their way over to the bench at the farthest end of the playground. There they sat, knees pressed together, giggling and poring over Simon's comic books. I stood at the window, just staring at them. At four years old I had the nerve to be jealous. I watched as Simon handed his comics to a beaming Josephine, and when the bell finally signalled the end of break time, the two of them stood up, little Josephine slipped one of her seven-year-old arms through his, and they walked back to class.

Even today, decades later, it doesn't take much for me to recall that excruciating pang of first love unrequited – I think because the *feeling* of love, and love *lost*, never really changes. Four or 40, for me, love – the falling *into* part – has always felt the same. Isn't it only our perspective that changes, rather than the feeling? Our understanding of who we are, what love sounds and tastes like, and where and who it comes from?

In pursuit of unconditional, unwavering, all-consuming love,

I have often lost myself to it. The unrequited, unattainable, impermanent, often impossible version of it. I have always fallen fast, and loved hard and with my whole heart. It's probably true to say that the first thing I was ever addicted to was love, or at least the idea of what I thought love ought to be. Way before I ever sought solace in eating too little or eating too much, medicating nonexistent back pain and toothache with pills or drinking away my emotional *einas* with gin and bottles of cheap rosé, I fell in love with the *idea* of falling in love, with the same hunger, the same compulsion, with which a junkie chases his next score.

At least part of the blame for why I've always held such unrealistic expectations of what love should look and feel like must lie with the books I devoured as a child. Like so many of us who find ourselves using unhealthy ways to avoid reality, burying myself in books was one of my earliest means of escape. From the time I could read, I did so obsessively, to the delight of my proud parents and schoolteachers. Because it seemed to be a good thing, I never dared let on the anxiety that seemed to well up inside me when I *didn't* have a book in my hands, a story to lose myself in and characters to befriend and root for. Ironically, despite all the reading, I still didn't have the words to explain the need I had to dive between the pages of a book to escape the noise of life. Of real life.

The books I loved the most were ones that featured till-death-us-do-part love stories. Ones where the couples ended up together against the odds. Where star-crossed lovers traversed oceans, slayed dragons, battled armies and survived dread disease to be together. Whatever trials and tribulations they faced, nothing was ever too much for their love to overcome. The power of "*I love you*" was infinite.

These stories *always* had happy endings. Love would *always* save the day. And that was my downfall. I bought into it completely. Everything I saw painted love as unconditional. There was nothing you wouldn't do for someone if you loved them. Truly loved them. Love meant enduring, suffering, burning-the-soles-of-your-feet-on-hot-coals-let-no-man-put-asunder-type love. *"There's nothing we can't survive if we love each other, right, baby?"* And I fell for it – hook, line and sinker. I was not able to differentiate between fact and fantasy. I took it all as gospel and couldn't wait for the day when someone would love me with the same intensity and determination as the characters in my books. I believed that it was not a case of *if* a love like that was possible and coming my way, but rather *when* it would fall into my lap. I fantasised about a love that was fireproof and watertight. Indestructible and unconditional. As far as I was concerned, Lennon and McCartney had it right on the money when they said "love is all you need".

2

Enver

There's a type of love – the type I fell into with Enver – that doesn't have the decency to announce itself. It happens upon you, almost violently, without the whiff of prospect or a shred of embarrassment. It is unapologetic and determined. It is live, sentient. It is love as an organism. It is addictive. It is love as addiction.

He was walking down a narrow hallway towards me the first time I saw him. A hallway in The Clinic. I'd been sent there from the rehabilitation centre I'd checked into five months before in an attempt to beat my eating-disorder demons and their band of troublesome companions. Despite rattling with a concoction of daily meds, I was still deeply depressed, the suicidal thoughts that had plagued me for too many of my 27 years scratching at the back door again, like a relentless, determined black dog.

In rehab I had begun the excruciating process of peeling back layers of hurt, and the wounds exposed during treatment had left me raw. All the rot I'd been trying to bury with food and pills and booze and mad, bad love in the hope it would simply disappear was being laid bare, and the only thing left to do was confront it – and I didn't think I could do that.

I'd started self-harming again – a coping mechanism that had begun in childhood – and, as a result, the rehab decided it could no longer "contain" me. They told me I would have to leave until it was under control, until I no longer posed a serious risk to myself. I'd be sent to The Clinic, a nearby psychiatric facility where I was immediately put on suicide watch and my belts, cigarette lighters, dressing-gown cord and other potential dangers were confiscated and placed under lock and key.

Despite the precautions taken by the nurses, I spent the first few days butchering myself with a blade I'd hidden in my hair before leaving the rehab. I was able to do some pretty ugly damage before I was caught by one of the night staff. From then on, showers and even using the bathroom had to be done with doors open. Every day my stitches would be cleaned, my wounds dressed, and every night I'd pick at them until they ran livid and vivid red again. In my daily sessions with my psychiatrist, I would sit staring into nothing, as if existing only behind a pane of glass. Years of training myself how not to feel finally paying off. That was one of the lowest points of my life.

Enver had arrived five or six weeks into my 10-week stay at The Clinic. He was admitted for just two weeks. To detox. From heroin. Enver didn't look like a heroin addict. He looked like a model. Like he belonged in the glossy pages of a fashion magazine, gliding down a runway. In the split second we passed one another in the hallway, I had taken in all of him. Impossibly high cheekbones, sturdy shoulders shrouded in a navy T-shirt, a comfortingly broad chest. Forearms that made me forget myself, long, slim fingers and endlessly long legs wrapped in indigo-blue denim.

Enver had the gait of young man who, at 24, had yet to discover his own true power, yet he moved as if at any second he might fall into it and stride through the rest of his life like he had known it and held it forever. But there was also a sense that he was a man on the precipice of himself. That his next step could either be to march determinedly forward to claim a life rich in purpose and passion and pride or instead, as too

23

many addicts do, to step askew and topple over the rim of the precipice and into the abyss with no guarantee of survival.

Something changed in me in the second we passed in that hallway. For the first time in months, I felt a flicker of something. Something hopeful. Seeing Enver on the knife's edge of two very different possibilities reminded me that there is always another choice. There is always something else. For good, for bad. Enver was a reminder that life could at once be both terrifying and beautiful. And in that finger snap of a moment, at what was the bleakest of times, the person I *had* been instantly and without fuss or fanfare edged sideways ever so slightly to make room for someone else. A someone whose default switch wasn't always set to "Dark". Enver gave me hope. Enver made me want to live. And for that, I loved him instantly. He literally became the love of my life. Enver *saved* my life.

From that moment there would always be a part of me that had Enver in it. Even though not a word, and barely even a glance, had passed between us, a dialogue had begun that spelled out how we would be inextricably linked for years and lives to come.

It was a couple of days later, in the dining hall, that we exchanged our first words. Our meet-cute in the Cuckoo's Nest. Both seated at the same long dining table, a single chair between us. Me determinedly starving the flesh off my bones, refusing anything except minuscule mouthfuls of wilting lettuce and tepid water, him devouring plate after plate of powdery roast potatoes, overcooked vegetables and anaemic-looking meat.

"You need to clear your plate from the table – this isn't your mother's house," I'd quipped as he stood up from the table, still chewing, and left his empty plate behind to head for the coffee station. Unsure of how he might respond, I kept my eyes front, pushing chunks of grey chicken around my plate. The prospect that he might either laugh or tell me to go fuck myself excited me. It felt good to feel excited. It felt good to feel. As it was, he did neither; instead, he picked up his plate and threw me a shy smile that, had I been standing, would have taken my knees out.

"Sorry, Sara-Jayne."

Two days later we kissed for the first time. Huddled in the doorway of my bedroom. Our feet touching, toes together, teetering on the edge of the rules that forbade male patients from entering the rooms of female patients. I remember being aware, as we'd moved towards each other, of this being the first time I'd really seen his face. Up close, I mean. Until then it had always been from afar, stolen glimpses across the TV room in the evenings or side glances in the garden where we sat together puffing smoke clouds and inhaling cups of cat-piss coffee. Up close, he was striking, beautiful. When he moved in closer, our eyelashes practically touching, I realised he had the darkest eyes I'd ever seen.

In my journal that evening I wrote: *There is someone. Gentle. Beautiful. When he leaves the room, I feel lonely.*

Enver would later confide that he'd actually spotted me *before* that lightning-flash moment in the hallway. On the day he arrived, he'd been sitting outside the nurses' station with his mother, waiting to be checked in. He was high. I'd emerged from a session with my psychiatrist, my arms bandaged from wrist to elbow. He said I looked "beautiful and sad". After that, he said, he intentionally sought me out. He would watch me, sitting outside the nurses' station waiting for medication, alone in the garden, chain-smoking Marlboro after Marlboro, and in front of the television, curled into the arm of the vast, faux-velvet couch, staring sadly at the flickering screen.

Initially, when he confessed he'd been watching me, I thought it was the most romantic thing I'd ever heard, but years later, during darker times, I would wonder whether in fact the watching was more like *hunting*, the way a predator does its prey.

Because he was detoxing, Enver wasn't required to participate in the daily group sessions and I had been deemed too "fragile" to attend and so, for the next few days, he and I spent all our time together. Mostly, we would sit outside in the garden, under the enormous tree whose branches tapped indecipherable Morse code on my bedroom window at night. We talked, we smoked, we laughed. Sometimes we simply sat in silence, fingers interlaced, gazing up through the rustling green canopy above our heads. In these quiet, simple moments, I began to be seduced by the prospect of living and loving life again. How could I want to die when the world had Enver in it?

In the evenings, after supper, we would join the other patients in the TV room, me reluctantly sharing Enver's beauty with the other crazies. Nestled thigh to thigh on the couch, I would lean into the safety of his armpit while he draped a protective, possessive arm along the back of the sofa and across my shoulders. Every so often we would manage to steal a kiss and I could feel the warmth creeping slowly back into my bones.

The fact that the rules of The Clinic clearly stipulated that there was to be no fraternising between patients was of no concern to either of us – nor, it seemed, to the clinic staff who, I later discovered, were not turning a blind eye to our relationship as I had believed, but, in fact, encouraging it. For weeks prior, the soft, kind nurse angels had been watching me break and bleed. Helpless spectators to my deterioration. But since Enver's arrival, they had seen my mood and mental state improving daily.

"Keep talking to her," they suggested to him. "It's making her better." And so he did – and it was. In fact, I was so captivated by Enver and by our connection that it took a while for me to notice that I was no longer being accompanied everywhere by a nurse. Being with Enver reminded me what it was like to feel happy, joyful and unburdened. To not have the constant weight of sorrow spoiling the promise of a new day and the safe retreat of the night.

Every evening I looked forward to going to sleep because it held the assurance that in the morning I would see him again, always as if it were the first time. It no longer hurt to breathe. Cracks began appearing in the glass that had been keeping the world out and I stopped picking at my wounds and allowed them to become scars.

From the moment we met, Enver became my love story, my *life* story – that was how I saw him. The love of my life. I genuinely believed we were *meant* to be together. That it was preordained. The love I had for him was the strongest force I had ever consciously known. He was the lead in my real-life romance novel and there *could* only be a happy ending. After all, I reasoned, love is all that matters. Love is the end and the beginning. I never thought to question the *why* of us. It was enough to know that Enver could turn the dark into day and that the universe *must* have put him in my path for a reason. For a long time, the only answer I would accept to the question of *why* was ... *love*.

3

And then there were three

In the bathroom of the Drostdy Theatre in Stellenbosch, I pee on a stick and become a mother. It's a Friday in March. I'm 38.

I've driven out to Stellenbosch for a literary festival, to speak to a bunch of middle-aged *boekliefhebbers* about my book, *Killing Karoline*, and do a couple of interviews where I'll probably pretend that I hate talking about myself and being asked how it feels to be brave and brilliant.

Pregnant. At 12:11pm. I scramble for my phone and quickly snap four pictures of the test – pffft, pffft, pffft, pffft. The digital indicator reckons about three weeks. It even says "Pregnant". I look in the mirror and laugh, "That explains the eggs."

Every morning Enver cooks me eggs. I've long told myself that cooking is his love language. The eggs are usually boiled, sometimes scrambled, and, if I'm honest, usually too dry. Nonetheless, I always happily inhale them, along with the weak tea with honey he makes in the oversized black mug with the chip in the handle and the red hearts I painted myself another lifetime ago. Recently, though, I've baulked at the thought of runny yolks and par-cooked albumen and settled for dry toast instead.

By some measure of I'm not sure which relationship scale, things are good between us. Life is our dance floor and we're gliding across it in our familiar waltz. Every day for two years we've done our best impression of two functioning adults in a functioning adult relationship. One-two-three-step, back two-three-step, twirl-two-three-step, side-two-three-step. It's a dance we've been doing for so long that, despite the fact we're actually just spinning around and around in the same spot, we don't even get dizzy. Not any more. Neither one of us has even noticed that the music has stopped playing.

Enver has finally managed to find a job and for the last few weeks has been leaving early in the morning to travel the 20-or-so kilometres to work where he puts in a hard day's slog for a hard day's pay. Except that most days I help him out with transport and cigarette money because he's waiting to be officially placed on the payroll and hasn't received a paycheque yet. When he does, he promises, he'll take me out for a romantic dinner where I'll have the salmon and he'll have the steak.

At the Drostdy, grinning from my occupied belly, I shove the stick into my bag, where it makes itself at home among the detritus of origamied petrol receipts, discarded chewing-gum wrappers and flecks of tobacco that have escaped from two half-smoked boxes of Marlboros I always have with me. On my way out of the theatre, I message Enver and tell him I want us to go to dinner tonight. "My treat," I say, as if another option exists.

The pregnancy is a surprise. To both of us. Not because we haven't been trying, because we have. Three weeks ago we (or had it been me?) had decided it was time.

"Neither of us is getting any younger," I'd joked, tugging at his belt, and since then we've been at it like rabbits and now our "hopping" has paid off. It is still a surprise though because we were both convinced – Enver silently and me outwardly – that the war I've been raging against my own body since I was 12 would eventually see my womb emerge the victor and declare itself unsuitable for foetal inhabitation. There's also the fact that I'm old, according to the internet, and as a "geriatric mother" I've been entirely prepared to wait at least a year or so for our non-stop boning to yield any results. But it's taken one go. The night of the morning we decided to start trying. Would you look at that!

Later that afternoon, with the positive pregnancy test zipped safely into my bag, I leave Stellenbosch and head back to Cape Town, where I fetch Enver from his mother's house and, in a staggering feat of spectacular and uncharacteristic self-control, manage not to blurt out right then and there on the stoep that I'm carrying his child. I wait until we're seated in the restaurant.

While Enver's studying the menu, I try, surreptitiously, to reach down into my bag and pull out my surprise. He's oblivious to the fiddling going on under the table, still vacillating between the rump and the rib eye. A defunct phone charger has the test in a stranglehold. Eventually, I haul everything out in a tangled heap and hurriedly slide the stick across the table.

"What's this?" he asks, confused.

I say nothing, but I'm smirking like an idiot.

"What?" He leans forward, narrowing his eyes.

"Look!" I point excitedly, tapping the stick with my forefinger. "Pregnant!"

He looks up at me and for a second I struggle to read his face, but then his brow furls and he bursts into tears. My own heart bursts. I've made him so happy.

We spend the remainder of dinner and the drive home talking excitedly about the baby and how the next seven or eight months will pan out. I mention how I'd like to cut back on the number of hours I've been working, having put in seven days a week for more than a year now, and Enver agrees. His job, although in its early days, seems secure and when the accounts department finally gets its act together next month, his salary will definitely help. He's also in the process of reviving his late father's business, something he's always wanted to do, and he's already been approached to throw his hat in the ring for a lucrative tender. I've helped him by lending him the money needed to register the business.

We even talk about the possibility of me giving up work entirely after the baby is born and, although being a stay-at-home mother has never really appealed to me, the thought of taking a break from the relentless, overworked, underpaid slog of the last 18 months is certainly alluring. Truth be told, it would be lovely to be looked after for a while. I try not to go on about it, but it's been tough holding the financial fort on my own for so long. Plus – although I'd never say as much to Enver because I know he's trying his best – to have yet another birthday or Christmas go by without even a small gift from him would be pretty bloody miserable. I'm longing for our relationship to stop existing on the water's edge of normal. I want us to dive in and start swimming.

The baby isn't the only big life event we're embarking on either; we're also just about to buy a house. Not really "we", though, since Enver doesn't have any money and has only just managed to find work, but thanks to my constant working and a sizeable cash injection from the Bank of Mum, I've just had an offer accepted on a modest two-bedroom cottage in the suburbs. It's in a dodgy neighbourhood and a whole heap of unsightly Vibracrete away from my dream home, but it's time and we'll make it work because we're about to have a baby, after all, and the fairy tale wouldn't be the fairy tale if we didn't first have to face a few bumps in the road along the way.

Because I want to do everything right and by the book and be the perfect mother to the perfect baby with the perfect partner, I make an appointment with my GP straightaway for a check-up. He takes some blood, gives me a general once-over and confirms that I am indeed expecting and about three weeks along. I find myself an obstetrician and schedule my first scan. I sign up to endless mom-to-be websites and newsletters and alerts and apps, including one that tells me every week how big the baby is, using pictures of fruit as a comparison. It seems impossible that in a few short months the three-week-old poppyseed floating around in my geriatric uterus will be pushing its way out of my 38-year-old vagina as a fully grown watermelon.

For the first few weeks of the pregnancy, life is strange. In some ways, it's a bit anticlimactic, and for the most part everything feels exactly the same as before. Apart from the handful of people we've told, the pregnancy is still a secret and because I'm still a long way away from showing, with the exception of the unrelenting morning sickness, it's business as usual.

But while there are moments when I completely forget there's a human growing inside me, there are also times when I feel a twinge or a cramp and I dash, panic-stricken, to the bathroom to check for bleeding. And although I can't always consciously connect to the fact that there is a baby growing inside me, the fear that a few ominous specks of blood might suddenly signal the end of the next chapter of our lives before it has begun renders me completely paralysed.

Every day, I'm green to the gills with morning sickness, which looks so inoffensive in all those rom-com she's-having-a-baby movies, but which in reality is a lot less like puking elegantly and noiselessly into a brown paper bag, a speckle of lady-like perspiration on my brow, and a lot more like unyielding nausea, sporadic dizziness and loud, ugly retching, head deep in the toilet bowl. Pretty soon it's not just eggs that have me gagging. It's any and all meats, dairy, fish, every single vegetable known to humankind and anything with even a whiff of wheat in it. I lose seven kilos in the first month of pregnancy, eating only watermelon and mango and sipping warm lemon water. The anorexic part of my brain, always lurking in the background in the hope of an invitation, thinks it's Christmas come early.

My aversions aren't limited to what I am (or am not) putting into my mouth. I'm also unable to cope with certain smells … including that of Enver. To me, he always smells *strange*. Metallic, bitter. His smoker's breath sends me reeling (I have, since learning I was pregnant, and thanks to Allen Carr, miraculously managed to quit my 24-year, 20-a-day habit) and when he breathes near me, I scrunch my nose, curl my lip and turn away dramatically. Sometimes when I'm feeling particularly rotten, I tut and snarl, "Urgh, can you just stop *breathing* on me!", which I'm allowed to do because I'm pregnant with his child.

We agree we'll keep our news to ourselves for now, although I'm so excited that I do share it with a few close friends *and* my mum, who seems surprised but not disappointed.

I'm a bit miffed that initially Enver seems reluctant to tell *his* mom – "Why *wouldn't* she be thrilled to become a grandmother again?" But I let the matter go, convinced that when we do eventually tell her, she'll be delighted to have another grandchild to dote on.

Then, a few days before my first scan, Enver shares our news with his mom. I'm not with him when he tells her, but when I ask about her reaction, all he will say is, "Ag, but you know my mom *mos*." I shake it off and try not to be too disappointed when I hear nothing from her by way of congratulations.

A couple of days later we take a rare trip to his moms's place for a family braai. Some of Enver's relatives are in town from overseas and it's been years since he last saw them. It only strikes me how seldom we visit on the occasions when we *do* actually visit. It never used to be that way, I think. In the early days of our relationship, we spent far more time there. These days, the ceremony of walking through the door and greeting whoever is inside always seems tinged with awkwardness, probably, again, because we're not regular visitors, or at least not me. Enver comes here when he and I are doing our "off-agains", but it's never for long. It always seems odd to me how my relationship with his family has never progressed beyond pleasantries and small talk, despite the length of time Enver and I have known each other. I commit, from my side, to making more of an effort, particularly in light of the baby, which obviously means we'll see a lot more of them.

By the time we arrive for the braai, there's a solid gathering at the house; we can hear it from the road as we pull up, park and make our way up the driveway. It's a large property and there are groups spread throughout. Hovering around the braai (men), in the kitchen (women), glued to phones and iPads in the back bedrooms (teens and tweens) and perched on chairs and wedged onto sofas in the living room and dining room. There's a general hubbub of goodwill and merriment. The news of the pregnancy has already been broken to certain family members ahead of our arrival and, once we arrive, an official confirmation is made, followed by back pats, hugs and glass clinks of congratulations as we make our way through the house.

It's such a big family, I think to myself later while gently fending off another offer of trifle. In a family *this* size, you can never be alone and, save for the international visitors, they all live close by. It's comforting. I'm happy but I also feel a pang of jealousy. My own family lives *so* far away (emotionally speaking, my mum and I live on different planets), and I feel their distance now more than ever.

At some point in the evening there is a call for a family photograph. Not really "family-family", I offer to take the picture, but someone shuffles me in next to Enver and in a flash we're saying "Cheese!" and getting ka-chick, ka-chick, ka-chick'ed into the portrait.

We leave the party with me on something of a high. While

Enver drives us home, I open his phone and look at the group photo already posted on Facebook by one of his relatives. There I am, carrying our baby, slap bang in the middle of the picture. Surrounded by people. What a lucky kid, I think, resting my hand on my belly, to be born into such a big, loving family.

4

Plant, pet, person

Just as soon as Enver had strode into my life at The Clinic, he was gone. For him, being there was a means to an end: to get the H out of his system. Once he was clean, he headed straight to a facility upcountry for a year-long treatment programme. We had only maybe 10 days together in total from the time he arrived until the time he left.

He had been in rehab once before, and his parents were taking no chances. The facility he was going to was a notoriously hardcore rehabilitation centre some 800 kilometres from Cape Town run by Christian zealots, known for using questionable methods to "cure" people of their addictions. If praying away the demons didn't work, there were always other more forceful, hands-on methods.

As sad as I was to say goodbye to Enver, all the love songs I'd ever listened to told me that all I had to do was wait and my love would come back to me, as if he'd never left. Initially, I wrote to him every day. Long letters detailing the minutiae of my days at The Clinic. What I did, who I saw and (miraculously now) what I ate. It was my way of staying connected to him. But after he'd been gone for about a month, my therapist took me aside to say she had received a letter from the head of the facility where Enver was and that he would only be given my letters in a few months' time.

"*Enver is focusing on his treatment programme,*" it read. "*Relationships in early recovery are always actively discouraged because relapse is most likely to happen in the first 12 months of getting clean. These early days are very important and should be devoid of any distractions. We suggest you also concentrate on your recovery.*"

This was the standard treatment-centre response, and they were quite right. The roller-coaster of emotions one experiences when first living without the crutch of drugs, booze or *any* addiction is the perfect kindling for even the slightest spark of temptation that might send you back into the lion's den. In the same way patients with broken bones are told to avoid stress on the injured area until it's healed, addicts are told to give it at least a year before embarking on a relationship. "Anything you put before your recovery you will lose."

Sensing my disappointment, my therapist offered some advice by way of an adage that has come to be adopted as an unofficial rule of recovery: the "plant, pet, person" rule.

"It's understandable that you're disappointed," she explained, "but if this relationship with Enver is to work, you both need to be well and emotionally strong enough. Get a plant – if the plant's still alive after a year, get a pet. If the pet's still alive after a year, *then*, maybe, you can begin to think about dating."

While I wasn't about to commit to the lives of either flora or fauna, I did, in the 12 months that Enver was gone, determinedly set about getting well. I had something to live for and threw myself into my recovery as if my life depended on it, which it did.

A couple of weeks after he left The Clinic, I was deemed well enough to return to my original rehab centre where I would complete the programme, move to the secondary living facility and then, eventually, into an apartment by the sea with one of the girls with whom I'd shared a room.

For a year I floated on the pink cloud of recovery. In the mornings I would meditate, go to the gym and take long walks along the seafront, inhale the ocean air and, through rose-tinted glasses, marvel at the beauty of the world. In the evenings, I would attend support meetings for a dose of 12-step wisdom, and in between I would write and hang out with my new recovery buddies. I just need to get better, I told myself. I'll get better, he'll get better and we'll be better together. I threw myself into my new sober life, excited to receive the rewards of recovery promised by the old-timers in the meetings but believing that Enver would be the real prize.

Eventually, after a few months, he was allowed to receive calls. Night after night we would talk on the phone, each of us smiling into our respective handsets, recapping the day's events, keeping each other up to date and counting down the months, then days, when we'd be back together.

A year to the day since he left, Enver came home. He looked incredible. Even better than before. He felt incredible too. My resolve to hold out on the physical aspect of our relationship at least for a few weeks after his return lasted only a couple of hours at best. A friend's mom had told me years before, "There's nothing more attractive than a reformed rogue" – and she was right.

With each new day we were together I found myself constantly marvelling that he had chosen me, that this beautiful creature was mine. Only a year into recovery, my self-esteem was still cripplingly low and while it wasn't that I didn't think I was good enough for Enver, I did frequently remind myself how lucky I was to have him.

The first couple of months after he came back, everything felt right with the world. I'd found myself a job writing for a travel company and he began working for his father in the family business. After work and at weekends we'd spend time at his parents' house or in my apartment cooking, watching movies and making love. We'd take road trips, my hand resting on his knee or squeezed between the underside of his thigh and the driver's seat. We talked endlessly of a future together. Marriage, babies and the white picket fence.

It was everything I'd dreamed it would be in the months Enver had been away. I marvelled at being able to be myself with him. He'd seen me at my worst, so there was no need for pretence. We were who we were and Enver, as I was learning, was a kind and sensitive soul, one of the gentlest people I'd ever met. He was considerate too, always making sure I was okay, always making me feel safe. We laughed constantly and the sex was spectacular. I'd also never met a man as attractive as Enver who didn't come with bucket loads of arrogance and entitlement. With other people, he could be quite shy, which was endearing. Everything between us was as I thought love was meant to be.

I was still attending daily recovery meetings and had built up a small but close circle of friends, also recovering addicts, committed to life without the crutches or chaos of booze, benzos and bingeing. I looked forward to the meetings where I could unburden myself and unload the day's events, good or bad, safe in the knowledge that everyone else in the room had, or was going through, similar highs and lows and plateaus.

I had assumed that when Enver came back, he too would attend the groups. Even before he was home, I'd created a fantasy in my mind that we'd skip along to meetings together, our love for recovery growing alongside our love for each other. We'd become known as Mr and Mrs Recovery; others would want what we had and, of course, we'd prove wrong the naysayers who had warned against our "rehab romance". I had it all planned out in my crazy head.

What I hadn't bargained for was that, despite being clean for a year, the brand of recovery Enver was now subscribing to was less about working the steps and more about stepping into the light of the Lord. His reluctance to attend meetings, get a sponsor or do the other things suggested for addicts in early recovery made me anxious and, as someone who had always struggled with any form of organised religion and baulked at the mention of Jesus or redemption, I bristled each time he would reassure me that "God has got this", but I was convinced he'd come around eventually. After all, it was unthinkable that either one of us would be prepared to give up the lives and the love that we'd waited for for so long. I had no doubt that Enver was as invested in "the dream" as I was. But the dream demanded work.

Enver had been home close to six months when I needed to fly back to the UK to tie up some loose ends. I still owned a house in London, and the time had come to sell it. I didn't *want* to go – as far as I was concerned, I would be quite happy to never return to England – but it made no sense to hang on to the house when my life was now in South Africa. The sooner I went, the sooner I'd be back, I reasoned.

Enver drove me to the airport. "It's only a few weeks," I reassured him as he pressed his lips against my forehead and told me how much he loved me. "And then we get to truly start our happily ever after."

I had no idea, as I walked through the gates at Departures, waving him a teary goodbye and promising to be back "in a few sleeps", that it would be nearly six *years* before I saw him again.

5

Be careful what you wish for

I'm just over nine weeks pregnant when we go for our first scan. It's the first time we're meeting my obstetrician. Years of bad experiences with white (usually male) health professionals means I've spent time painstakingly trying to find a doctor I'm comfortable with delivering my firstborn. I'm delighted and relieved to find someone who ticks almost every box of my "black, female, pro-vaginal birth" criteria. Dr Wondimu has an excellent reputation and makes me feel immediately at ease, even if he is not a she.

In the waiting room, Enver and I whisper to one another in the low, measured way people in waiting rooms tend to speak to each other. It starts off as arbitrary waiting-room chitchat – "cold in here", "pass me that leaflet", a childish giggle at the plastic cross-section of a uterus on the reception desk – but soon enough it turns to the baby. For weeks my mind has been brimming with hundreds of questions and I'm looking forward to getting some answers from Dr Wondimu. I ask Enver whether there's anything *he* wants to ask.

"No, not really," he says vaguely, making me instantly annoyed.

"Nothing?" I whisper incredulously. "There's *nothing* you want to ask the doctor who will be delivering our child?"

"No, SJ, I can't think of anything *right this second!*" he snaps back.

"And *prior* to this second, there was nothing you felt you might want to know?" I sneer.

Our voices are getting louder and I'm relieved when Dr Wondimu pops his head out of his office and we're forced to bury our agitation behind our can't-wait-to-be-new-parents smiles. I hate it when Enver is like this. Why is he trying to ruin this special day?

The fight is forgotten a few minutes later when I'm lying on the examination table, holding my breath and looking at a grainy image of a tiny, jelly-baby-like blob on a computer screen.

"And there's your baby," says Dr Wondimu kindly, smiling at the screen.

It is the single most extraordinary moment of my life. Mine. My flesh, my blood. I exhale and burst into tears. I feel Enver's hand slide into mine and grip, hard. He's also crying. "Is he okay?" he asks, his voice trembling, and then before Dr Wondimu has the chance to reply, answers his own question with "He's fine, he's fine" and nodding as if trying to reassure himself.

"Yes," says Wondimu, "there's your baby and it's fine. Beautiful. Would you like to hear the heartbeat?" We both nod enthusiastically through the sobs and a second later the room is filled with du-dum du-dum du-dum. More sobs.

Enver squeezes my hand more tightly and kisses me on the forehead.

"He?" I laugh through the tears. "It might be a girl!"

"As long as it's healthy," says Enver. "As long as it's healthy and you're healthy."

We leave Dr Wondimu's office with a picture of our baby and a follow-up appointment in three weeks.

In addition to finding Dr Wondimu and becoming an expert on fruit babies, I've also started preparing for the baby's arrival.

I'm working out how long it will take to get to the hospital when I go into labour. I was never a Girl Scout or anything, but I'm a firm believer in being prepared. Preparation is everything. Expect the best, prepare for the worst. I'm still working on the first part. A therapist once told me that obsessive preparedness is actually hyper-vigilance – common, she'd said, in people who've suffered trauma or had a dysfunctional childhood. I just know I like to be prepared and in control. Just in case.

I've made note of several calculations and routes to the hospital from the new house (both during and outside rush hour), from the gym, from Enver's mom's house (I was serious about spending more time there) and from the radio station where I work, should I, God forbid, go into labour while hosting my late-night talk show. I'm literally covering all avenues. One thing I definitely *don't* want when it comes to this pregnancy is any nasty surprises.

Enver appears less enthusiastic about the logistic planning and seems to hover on the peripheries of all the new-house admin (of which there is a lot), but I suppose that makes sense since it is *my* house and, so far, my money funding the whole operation. Enver's promised that when he eventually gets paid (inexplicably, there's *still* an issue with his salary at the now not-so-new-job) he'll start contributing. It's a small firm, granted, but surely even the lowest-ranking Accounts personnel aren't *this* incompetent? I can't understand why Enver isn't making more of an issue about it, but I also get it: "SJ's got us covered." Still, he says that when the money *does* eventually come through, *he'll* pay for the rather pricey new wooden floor I'm having put in. I smile and say, "Thanks, love."

He also talks a lot about all he will do at the house once we're in. Practical things, *man* things, things requiring spirit levels and robust biceps. I'm grateful that I will have him around to help with the heavy lifting and, of course, the decorating of the spare room, which I've rather haughtily started calling The Nursery.

Things have, however, been a bit rocky since our appointment with Dr Wondimu. I'm feeling unsettled. I'm not sure whether it's the hormones of early pregnancy, the stress of the house purchase, the endless slog at work or the fact that we're trying to manage several of *Cosmopolitan's* Top 10 Most Stressful Life Events all at once. After a fight with Enver one afternoon, a thought does its best to creep into my consciousness – *I didn't think it would be like this* – and then another – *Be careful what you wish for* – but it's too much to ponder, so I remind myself that pregnancy, indeed *life*, isn't like the movies and all that matters is that we're healthy, having a baby and on our way to everything we've ever wanted.

Enver also seems stressed. Not all the time; he's up and down, much like his mood. He's also putting in long hours at work and trying to get the new business up and running. I sometimes wonder whether I'm putting too much pressure on him or being too needy. Past experience means I'm always apprehensive of things taking a bad turn. Terrified of history repeating itself. "You've every right to be suspicious," I tell myself.

It's not that I think he would actually *take* drugs again, not after everything that's happened, and of course it would be unthinkable now because we've got a *baby* coming, but we addicts have to be vigilant. Wary of the "people, places and things" that trigger us. Careful not to get "hungry, angry, lonely or tired", the usual red flags.

I hate it when things are like this between us. When there's a disconnect. I also hate that we don't have the opportunity to spend much quality time together. Something's always getting in the way. I blame work. That's what's creating this sense of distance. As soon as his salary situation is sorted and I can ease up on my hours, it'll be different, I promise myself one evening while I'm waiting for him to get back from work. He's been coming home later and later at night and often, when he does get home, he's exhausted and ends up sleeping on the couch.

Until one night, when he doesn't come home at all.

6

Somebody that I used to know

February 2013, London

Time is a strange thing, I think to myself after his first message pings into my inbox. Minutes can be enough for one to have lived a million different lives, while years can be too short to even blink or catch one's breath.

It has been five years since I left Enver in Cape Town for my "quick trip" to England. Before I'd gone, promises had been made. Mine to fly back in just a few short weeks so he and I can continue our meant-to-be, his to wait for me. But, without follow-through, promises are just words and I'm shocked *beyond* words when, one day, after more than half a decade of radio silence, Enver flies back into my life, completely unannounced.

A message lights up my Twitter inbox early one morning. A bolt out of the blue bird. I'm at work, heading up the news team at a radio station in London, when I see the notification and his name appears on my screen.

Enver: SJ, HOW THE HELL ARE YOU?

"Fuck. Me."

One of the younger, greener journalists in the newsroom looks up from his desk. He's new enough in the game to have his ears still pricked up by expletives.

Fuck. Me.

Enver: I HAVE SO MUCH TO SAY TO YOU.

Fuck. Me

Enver: WANTED TO SAY THAT I'M REALLY SORRY ABOUT EVERYTHING.

Fuck.Me.

Enver: IF YOU EVER WANT TO TALK, LET ME KNOW.

"Fuck me!" someone shouts from across the room. "Oscar Pistorius has killed his girlfriend!"

Bang. Bang.

SJhowthehellareyouIhavesomuchtosaytoyouWantedtosay-thatImreallysorryabouteverythingIfyoueverwanttotalkletme-know.

"They're saying he shot her."

How the hell am I?

"What's the dialling code for South Africa?"

I'm knocked for a fucking six, that's how the hell I am.

"No idea, ask SJ ... SJ, what's the dialling code for South Africa?"

2-7.

If I ever want to talk.

"It's 2-7."

I always want to talk.

"SJ, it's two minutes to the top of the hour – are we running with this?"

Talking is what I do.

"One minute to, SJ ..."

It's what I get paid to do. So, sure, let's talk, because I have a lot to say ... Or do I?

"Okay, so we're leading with the Blade Runner, Grammys to finish, right? Right, SJ?"

The radio clock above the studio door flashes its red, 60-second countdown.

Time to talk.

"Uh, yeah, Pistorius, dead girlfriend, Grammys, got it."

Twenty-seven seconds.

"They're saying she was planning on leaving him, some saying she'd already left."

Fuck. Me.

Headphones on, mic up, and ... live.

"It's 10 o'clock, I'm Sara-Jayne King and these are your latest headlines."

Talk about timing.

"We're getting reports from South Africa that Paralympian Oscar Pistorius is being held on suspicion of murdering his live-in girlfriend ..."

If she'd already left, why the fuck did she go back?

I make it through the rest of the bulletin on autopilot.

"And finally, the 55th Grammy Awards took place in Los Angeles last night. Gotye was the big winner of the evening, taking the award for Record of the Year for 'Somebody That I Used to Know'."

The other thing about time is that it can alter some things beyond all recognition, while it can leave others entirely unchanged, exactly as they were and always will be. What hasn't changed for me, I realise on receiving his message, is that I know I still love Enver. But that love has acquired some tricky sidekicks – anger, mistrust and disappointment – because of what happened five years before. What he did to us. What he did to me. What he did to himself.

When I'd left Cape Town for England five years previously, my intention was to get back as quickly as possible. I wanted to get home to Enver as soon as I could so that we could start writing the next chapter of our love story. I had it all mapped out. As soon as I was back, I would find a job and rent a small flat. We wouldn't live together, not immediately. It would be important in the early years of our recovery and relationship for us to continue to focus on our individual journeys, getting to know *ourselves* and not risk falling into codependency or an unhealthy attachment to one another (I'd read an *awful* lot of Louise Hay in the months since leaving rehab).

Even though we would live separately, Enver would keep a toothbrush (blue) next to mine (pink) in the toothpaste-spattered cup in my bathroom and, on the occasions he spent the night (twice a week, max), he'd draw hearts in the steam on the mirror while I showered and I'd gently rib him about leaving the toilet seat up.

I'd clear out a space in my chest of drawers where he could keep some underwear, a couple of T-shirts and a hoody that I'd wear when he wasn't there. On Saturday morning, my neighbours would greet him with a knowing smirk when they spotted us unloading my weekly grocery shopping from the car and say things like, "There they go, the lovebirds," and we'd grin back bashfully.

I'd finally write that book I'd always talked about (even though it would probably never get published) and Enver would work for his dad while studying part-time to become an addictions counsellor. Eventually, in three or four years' time, in a storybook proposal – simple (but not *too* simple) and romantic in equal measure – Enver would ask me to be his wife and I, of course, would say yes. Three impossibly beautiful children would eventually follow, a boy and twin girls, and we'd live happily, happily, blah, blah, blah, the Volvo, the townhouse, the pool guy, the two Labradors, the forever-after-for-always. The end.

But life had got in the way of the love story.

I'd been in England for about three weeks. It was a Saturday evening, and I'd just got back from my regular NA meeting. I was coming up for two years clean, but still early days as far as recovery goes. Throughout my 10 months in rehab it had been drilled into me that the hardest part of my recovery was yet to come. "*Getting* clean and sober is easy; it's *staying* clean and sober that's hard." The message I heard over and over again was to go to meetings, get a sponsor and work the steps if I wanted to not only stay clean but also start living and enjoying life as opposed to just surviving it. The glimmer of what was promised if I focused on my recovery had me completely convinced, so I did what was suggested.

In the meetings, I really felt as if I had found my tribe: other addicts, people committed to recovering from whatever it was that had brought them to their knees. Day after day, I'd see people who had once lost everything to their addictions now living lives beyond their wildest dreams. People who sat together in church halls and Scout huts, community centres and correctional facilities and created safe pockets in which to cry and rage and recover. People learning to love themselves enough to live. I wanted what they had, and Enver, and the life we had planned together, was the pot of gold I believed was waiting at the end of my recovery rainbow.

I also came to see pretty quickly that, as hard as recovery was – and some days were really brutal – it was a shit-ton better than how my life had been before. I vowed never to take for granted the gift of recovery and took seriously the warning about losing anything I prioritised over it.

Because I was convinced that Enver would *eventually* come around to the idea of attending meetings too, I decided not to push him. Attraction rather than promotion, people in the meetings would tell me. "Be the example." But his avoiding meetings did make me anxious. I'd never heard of a success story of any addict who'd stopped taking drugs and, just like that, without any further action, managed to lead a healthy, happy, clean and sober life. The knot in my stomach always wound a little tighter when Enver told me that he didn't need "all that stuff". Recovery, as I had been taught, wasn't just about abstinence – it was about *healing*, filling the cracks, rather than trying to paper over them.

The other thing that bothered me was Enver's insistence that the *only* monkey on his back was heroin. Too often over the past two years I'd heard other drug addicts in early recovery tell themselves the same thing. They'd swear their problem was only with the hard stuff, street drugs, not things like weed ("C'mon, I mean, it's basically a vegetable") or booze ("It's the drugs I've got to stay away from, one *dop* won't do me any harm") only to wind up worse than before, after "just one beer" or "a few puffs" of a joint. The slippery slope always meant that they found themselves back on their asses in the end.

Even though I had been in recovery for nearly two years, I was still an addict and the denial in me was still strong. I could refuse to see something even when it was in front of my nose, and to give too much space to my concerns about Enver left me with a tight sensation in my chest that got in the way of my ability to exhale. It had taken me 29 years to find a love like this, and I wasn't about to give it up for something that might not even happen. For the most part, I pushed my doubts to the back of my mind and even (subconsciously, I think) doubled my own recovery efforts as if that might ensure there was enough healing to share between the two of us. Recovery by proxy.

When he answered the phone that Saturday evening, I could immediately tell that Enver wasn't at home. The hubbub in the background was peppered with clinking glasses, the odd ripple of laughter, a muffled cacophony of voices but none distinct enough to actually make out what anyone was saying. I was glad he was out and reconnecting with some of the people from his life before addiction had dug in its claws.

So far in our relationship, Enver and I had spent very little time with other people. I had my small clique from rehab and the meetings, and we were often at his parents' house, but we didn't really socialise beyond that. One of the reasons was that we were so infatuated with each other that we had little regard for anything or anyone else. Another was that, save for the acquaintances with whom he'd used drugs, all Enver's friends had moved on. They were ambitious young 20-somethings, busy furthering their careers, getting married, going overseas, having kids. They were living. That's another thing addiction does to you – it makes sure you get left behind.

So I was pleased that Enver was socialising. I didn't want us to become one of *those* couples. Couples who only ever want to be together, all the livelong day, forsaking all others and all other invitations to experience life outside their relationship. Couples who finish each other's sentences and suck on either end of the same strand of spaghetti at the local Italian restaurant they go to every single goddamn Friday night despite the fact that they've taken advantage of the two-for-one special and they each have their own fucking plate. I definitely did not want us to become *those* people.

The other thing I could tell immediately when Enver answered the phone was that he was drunk. Growing up in a house with an alcoholic makes one acutely aware of other people's behaviour under the influence. Particularly the behaviour of someone doing their best not to let on that they're wasted. Enver had failed.

"Hi, baby, everything okay?" I'd asked when it had taken him longer than usual to answer the phone.

"Hi, my baby girl, howwwzzzit going!" he boomed. He was practically shouting, his voice far louder than the background noise warranted.

Oh my God. Is he drunk?

"Enver, are you drunk?"

"What! You know ... *hic* ... I don' drink, baybeee!"

Oh my God. He's drunk.

"Enver. *Have you been drinking?*"

"I misssh you ssoo mushhh ... an' I can't wait to sheee you, my baby!"

This can't be happening.

I hated hearing the slur in his voice. Too many consonants pushed up against each other in their hurry to tumble out. Drunk Enver was conjuring up unwelcome flashbacks to my childhood and a home disrupted for years by my brother's loud, destructive alcoholism.

I'd been taught that at times of crisis I should lean into recovery. This could definitely be considered a crisis. What would my sponsor do? I decided she'd probably say the Serenity Prayer and, although I'm not even remotely religious and struggle with the concept of God, without knowing what else to do, I closed my eyes and started reciting the words in my head.

God.

"What's happening, why are you drunk, where are you?"

"Sshorrryy, I can' hear you too well, ssshweettheart."

Grant me the serenity.

"Why are you drinking, Enver?"

"Isss okay, I'm just with some friends. It's Ismail's wife's birthday."

To accept the things I cannot change.

"Who? Who's Ismail? What's going on?"

"Whaddya wearing? You soooo sssexy when you mad."

The courage to change the things I can.

"What the fuck, Enver! Why have you done this?"

"Itssssokaybabyitsallgoood!"

And the wisdom to know the difference.

The conversation lasted no more than three minutes. The

second the line disconnected, I let the phone fall out of my hand and slid slowly down the sofa where I sat slumped against it, my palms down on the floor either side of me. I felt safer down there. There's nowhere to fall if you're already on the ground. For 20 minutes I just sat there in disbelief. This *couldn't* be happening. The tears demanded their moment and I let them have it.

Eventually, after too long on the floor, I dried my wet face with my sleeve and ordered myself to stand. "Up!" I commanded, picking myself off the floor. The second I'd heard Enver slurring down the phone line, I knew I couldn't go back to Cape Town. Enver's relapse threatened my own sobriety and although my life was hardly perfect, if I lost that, I lost everything. Even though he swore he would stop, I knew that without the right support, things were likely to get worse.

But while the decision was easy, the fallout was hard. It took about four months for the relationship to die completely. Four months that, at times, I felt might break me. Having fought so hard all my life to find it, I couldn't bear the thought of having to let go. To let go of love. I so desperately wanted to fix, to convince, to beg, to cajole, to fly back to South Africa to remind Enver how good we had it and what he was giving up, but the voice of recovery was, at the time, miraculously louder than the voice of recklessness.

One day I was scrolling through Facebook when I noticed that Enver's sister had posted some new pictures. I clicked mindlessly through them. It looked like a weekend away, she and some friends. I kept clicking and soon wished I hadn't. There was a picture of Enver. He had a bottle of whiskey in his hand. In the next image he was laughing, the bottle at his mouth. I'd never seen his eyes like that. Glassy and unfocused. It felt like I was looking at a stranger, or someone I'd passed in the street once upon a time. The last picture was of Enver passed out drunk on a sofa, surrounded by empty bottles.

Soon after there were more photos, this time of a party at Enver's parents' house. There was Enver again, gorgeous as ever, smiling and laughing, with a beer in his hand. Even though it hurt my heart to do it, I kept scrolling through the images until one made my heart stop.

Enver standing behind a thin, very pretty but sullen-looking girl, his arms wrapped around her waist. She was younger than him, about 19 or 20. His fingers intertwined with hers and her right arm was crossed over his in a gesture of possession. Both were staring directly into the camera. They looked like beautiful, moody models. That was the end. The moment the last piece of my heart splintered. I shut down my computer and said goodbye to my happily-ever-after.

So when he tweets himself back into my life, five years later, I'm blindsided and I tell him so.

SJ: I don't know what to say, Enver. This has come as a complete shock.

Enver: I know. I'm really sorry for the blast from the past. Are you engaged? Seeing someone?

I'm not, but I don't tell him that. Not at first. There have been very few persons of interest since Enver. There was a guy I met at the meetings, but that never progressed beyond a few awkward coffee dates. There was also David, a roguish and emotionally unavailable Scotsman I'd first fallen head over heels for at university nearly 10 years prior but who had never been willing to take our relationship beyond the "friends with benefits" status. We'd resumed a dalliance of sorts about two years ago, but again it had never really got off the ground. Mostly I'd spent the last five years nursing a broken heart, focusing on my recovery, and getting my career back on track. And that's what I tell Enver.

Enver: You've made all the right decisions, while I made crazy ones.

No kidding.

From my side, I've done enough sporadic stalking over the years to know that Enver is no longer with the moody beauty from the pictures. I've also managed to deduce that, as I'd feared he would, he had ended up back on the smack after going back to the bottle. I'd been furious and also terribly sad when I found out. What a *waste*. Enver had so much going for him – I'd known it as soon as I'd met him. He had so much potential and such a truly good heart. But, without believing he deserved recovery, it would always remain beyond his grasp. The same reason so many addicts never get it. It made me so sad, and I often told him, "I wish you could see yourself through my eyes." I don't ask, but he volunteers the information that he's now clean.

I can't help but ask if *he* is seeing anyone.

Enver: I'm lonely, I'm unhappy … Whatever is happening in my life is not what I want.

SJ: What does that mean?

Enver: It means I want to move on from what's toxic in my life.

SJ: Okay, that means yes. Not cool, Enver.

Enver: People make mistakes.

SJ: Can't you just answer the question?

Enver: Okay, yes I am, but it's gone very bad, and we've drifted apart.

It happens. I choose to believe him.

Enver: So you're doing good?

SJ: I'm okay. A lot has happened in the past few years.

And it has. Despite things going well for me on the career front and the fact I'm still sober, I'm not really happy. I feel … incomplete. Since being back in England, I've also battled with my mental health and have seen the inside of more than one psychiatric facility in the last five years. I'm also really lonely.

Enver: Can I have your number? Can we talk?

I realise I want more than anything to hear this man's voice again.

Enver: I just want to hear your voice.

Damn it. I could never say no to Enver. I type out my number and hit Send. I'm getting closure, I tell myself. We never had that, and now's my chance to get it. It's a really convincing line.

SJ: Call me tomorrow. Am at work now. Can't talk.

Enver: Long-distance telephonic date! Looking forward.

SJ: NOT a date. A conversation between two people who once knew each other.

Enver: Just kidding! Don't want to be on your shit list, or am I already there?

SJ: Believe me, Enver, you're on that list.

Enver: And once you're on, you're fucked, right?

SJ: You know me too well.

The instant I hear his voice on the other end of the line the following day, all bets are off. My brain puts two and two together and comes up with Enver as the solution to my restlessness and discontent. He's saved me once before, and now, like a knight in shining armour, he's here to save me again. Just like in the love stories I'd read as a child, we were destined to be together, even if it meant first surviving the things designed to tear us asunder. And so, addicts that we are, we pick up, albeit long distance, right where we'd left off five years before.

For the next few months, I float around on an Enver high. We talk and text and email every day, fantasising about the future we'll have together once I'm back in South Africa. My plan had always been to return and my reconnecting with Enver is all the convincing I need that now is the right time.

There are red flags, of course, but I ignore them, so steadfast is my belief that Enver and I are meant to be and my determination that this time nothing will get in the way of our happy ending. I tell myself that the universe would not have brought him back into my life for no reason, and the reason *must* be for us to be together. I book a one-way ticket back to South Africa, arriving a few days before Enver's 30th birthday.

But when I get back to Cape Town, the Enver I think I know is AWOL.

7

The first of the signs

It's been two days since Enver failed to come home after work.

He'd left the house early (as usual), having borrowed R50 (as usual) and claiming he'd be working on site the whole day. I'd sent him a couple of WhatsApps during the morning, to which he hadn't replied. I'd tried calling him in the afternoon, but the phone had just rung and then gone to voicemail. I tried again 10 minutes later; the phone was off. Ten minutes after *that* it was back to ringing. At 4pm, I told myself not to be alarmed. By 5pm I was relieved I no longer had to try to focus on work *and* the father of my unborn child being MIA.

By 6pm I decided I'd give him another hour, and by 7pm I'd done what I never do and called his mother who, as always (although never rude), refused to engage beyond answering either yes or no to the question, "Is Enver with you?" He wasn't.

Fuelled by fear, my imagination kicked into overdrive and began scrolling through the various options that might explain where Enver was. The first was that he was lying unconscious in a ditch somewhere after a terrible accident in the work van. Then there was the unlikely possibility that he'd had a heart attack on site and was being defibrillated on a gurney. Maybe he'd been shot while acting the hero, intervening in a robbery or the mugging of an old lady?

There was one last option, so unthinkable that I chose to give it no conscious audience in my head, and that was that he was somewhere pulling heroin into his lungs while I nurtured his child in the space under my heart.

I had sensed something wasn't right about a week ago, but to confront it head-on for what it could be was too terrifying. Almost as if my mind, doing its best to protect me (and the baby) from the truth, wouldn't allow me to say out loud, the possibility of my worst nightmare coming true.

First, there'd been an incident in which he'd dropped me at work an hour or so before my late-night radio show and then, half an hour later, I'd seen him driving past the studio, heading in the *opposite* direction from home. Towards town. The sketchy part.

Later, when he'd come to fetch me and I asked him *why* he had been driving my car towards the sketchy part of town at 10:30pm, he denied it outright. Looked me dead in the eye and told me flat out it wasn't him. Only when I began to lose it, screaming, banging the dashboard like a woman possessed, did he come up with some spurious reason. My only option was to believe him. That's the thing about denial – it makes sure you *don't* have a choice.

Then, a few days later, after he had already left early for work, the estate agent called to ask if we could meet at the new house to tie up some loose ends. I agreed and, arriving a few minutes early, decided to grab a drink from a shop a couple of roads away.

Pulling up outside the corner store, I noticed a familiar figure walking down the road. Enver. Enver? What's he doing here? "What are you doing here?" I shouted senselessly into the windscreen and then drove up, very slowly, alongside him. Like a cop.

It was a strange neighbourhood. On one hand, it was made up of families, generations long and strong. Hard-working, religious folk who answered the call to prayer four times a day and whose front and back doors still hung wide open and welcoming, as they had done for decades. Grandmothers and aunts, raising the children of their children, talked to one another across low garden walls with babies on their hips, while inside fragrant pots bubbled and simmered on ancient stoves.

But among the neighbourliness and the *salaams* lurked another reality. Pockets of vice and rot had crept in, taken root and settled. Merchants peddled their wares, their own pockets swollen with the hope of the discontented who, day in and day out, sold their last (and too often someone else's last) for a false promise.

It was on these very streets where Enver had existed for years in his *other* life. The life he lived away from me. The one to which he gravitated when we were on a break from "us". A life I'd never actually seen him living but of which he would bring traces through the front door, like dirt on a pair of shoes, when he eventually came home. This neighbourhood, which we would soon call our own, had been home to Enver when over the years he sought to fix his own internal sense of homelessness and displacement in its dark corners.

As I pulled up alongside him, it suddenly dawned on me that once we moved here, temptation would be right on our doorstep. It would be like living next door to your husband's former mistress. Knowing that at any minute he might be lured back to her with memories of how it had felt between her hot thighs.

Pulling up the handbrake, I was reminded of the recovery idiom, "You sit in a barber's chair long enough, you're going to get a haircut." I wondered how long it would be before Enver would come home, unrecognisable, having succumbed to the barber's shears.

When his hip was parallel to my passenger door, I wound

the window down and called out, "What are you doing here?" Without skipping a beat, he replied affably, "Hey, love, you okay?" as if it were the most normal thing in the world that *I* was there and *he* was there and not at work where we'd both believed the other was. A real pro. Only someone who'd spent as long as I had searching his face for answers to impossible questions would have noticed his left eye flicker.

"What are you doing here?" I said again, trying to keep my voice steady.

"Work called. They don't need me in until midday," he replied, leaning down and beaming into the car, his dark eyes shining bright and big like enormous black diamonds.

"But what are you doing *here*?" I was frantic now.

"Just getting a drink," he said, completely ignoring my mounting hysteria. "Gonna head off to work now."

"Enver, you work six kilometres away! *Why. Are. You. Here?*"

For a moment, neither of us moved. He waited on the edge of a breath to see whether this would be the moment we *both* crashed over the cliff face. But I just couldn't ask the question that could have sent us barrelling face first on to the rocks below. I couldn't, because then the gig would be up for him and the game would be over for both of us. And the consequences of that were too grim. In the space of the silence, I realised I didn't want an answer. I blinked myself back into the moment, my eyes refocusing on the clock on the dashboard that had tick-tocked me into tardiness.

"I'm late," I sighed. "I'm here to meet the agent at the house."

"I'll come with you," he said energetically, jumping into the car uninvited and disarming me with a kiss on the cheek. I headed towards the new house feeling ambushed, but also relieved. It was unthinkable that I'd just drive off, leaving him wandering through this addict's paradise.

He'd worked his magic like a true conjuror, distracting me

with his razzle-dazzle, a fast tongue and sleight of hand. His deceit and my denial. A dangerous combination.

At home later that night, after the dust had settled, I asked Enver to take a drug test. I hated doing it and he knew it. It pissed all over the love-of-my-life mantra I'd been chanting for more than a decade.

"This is fucked!" I raged. "None of my friends have to get their partners to do this, Enver." I felt humiliated for him *and* me as he'd stood with his cock in a plastic beaker, the next breath of our lives to be determined by the integrity of his urine.

The test came back negative. If I *really* believed there was a chance it would come back any other way, I probably wouldn't have asked him to do it, but I also wanted *him* to know I was watching him closely. And I wanted to reassure myself that all this anxiety and suspicion was just my pregnancy brain making me paranoid.

So, following his disappearance the other night and after finally managing to get hold of him, it has become clear that Enver, as I had suspected, has been flying a little too close to the sun. He'd managed to explain away his overnight disappearance – "working late", "dodgy cell phone reception" – but admitted he'd been struggling recently. He even confessed in a text message that he'd had a "slip" – a couple of swigs of methadone, a synthetic opioid replacement used to treat heroin addiction; scary, but not irredeemable.

This revelation, while alarming, is a good sign, I think. Admitting you have a problem is the first step. I've decided to allow him that one indiscretion, but only if he promises (and he must *really* mean it this time) that he'll put his recovery first. He says he will.

Eager to capitalise on his willingness to get help, I broke the cardinal recovery rule and called Jimmy. Jimmy is Enver's *latest* sponsor, handpicked by me. Selected straight out of a candlelit circle of suitable candidates at an NA meeting I'd strongarmed Enver into a few weeks ago when my anxiety had begun to sneak its devil fingers around the softest part of my neck again. I knew it was frowned upon to intervene in the sponsor/sponsee relationship, but so is risking your sobriety and relapsing on smack when you're about to have a baby.

Sensing my desperation, Jimmy has offered to mediate a conversation between Enver and me at his house. We need him to help us move beyond the no-man's-land of miscommunication and distrust where we seem to have pitched our weather-beaten tent of a relationship. I hoped he might offer to see us in the evening after work because I'm worried about how much time Enver's had to take off from his job recently to come with me to doctor's appointments and to sort out the new house. With the baby on the way, we cannot afford for him to lose his job.

Enver's been at his mom's place since the night he went AWOL, so we've agreed to meet at Jimmy's. Jimmy has the Sara-Jayne seal of approval. He used to be a drug counsellor at the rehab I'd gone to 13 years ago. He was tough back then, I remember. Didn't suffer fools. Could sniff out junkie bullshit from a mile off. He's also a recovery old-timer. A serious base-head in his day, he's now more than 20 years off the drugs himself. Jimmy is the gold standard of sponsors. I, *we*, need Jimmy on our team. Jimmy will make it all okay. Jimmy will help me. Jimmy will fix Enver. Jimmy will save us.

I pull up outside his house and, with the engine still running, tap the Contacts tab on my phone.

SEARCH. I start typing *Spon* ... – a list pops up of possible options.

Bryan Sponsor

J sponsor

Jimmy SPONSOR (new)

Justin Spons NA

Musi Sponsor

Ashley (possible) sponsor

It's an impotent and futile directory of sponsors past. It's also hard, wake-the-fuck-up-and-smell-the-goddamn-coffee evidence (if I had the capacity to see it) of how *none* of my goading, coaxing, suggesting, manipulating, bribing, pleading, blackmailing, begging, sucking or fucking has ever, *ever* worked to get Enver to take recovery seriously.

It's also testament to the sheer number of phones that have mysteriously vanished while in Enver's charge over the last few years, forcing him to frequently commandeer mine. They disappear, he maintains, through a combination of carelessness (his) and criminal skulduggery (other people's). He's been the victim of the most wretched misfortune, having been mugged at least four times in the last year alone.

I tap *Jimmy SPONSOR (new)*, and he picks up almost immediately.

"I'm outside," I tell him and switch off the engine.

I can see he's still trying to end the call as he walks out to meet me.

"He's not here yet," he mouths exaggeratedly, walking towards the car.

I'm relieved. That'll give us time to work on our game plan, basically a relapse prevention. Jimmy will convince him – in a way that I have as yet been unable to – to really commit to his recovery. He must, or he'll come dangerously close to picking up the drugs again and that obviously can't happen because we're about to have a baby. I'm determined that by the time we leave Jimmy's place, Enver will be back on the right path. Not fixed, of course not, not yet. Recovery, after all, is a journey, not a destination.

I follow Jimmy inside, past two dust-dirty cats batting each other's paws back and forth in the driveway.

"Tea?" he asks as I perch on the edge of an impossibly low and uncomfortable sofa.

I nod too soon before he has time to add, "There's no milk, though." He pours boiling water onto a couple of stray teabags he's thrown into two grubby mugs and excuses himself to go to the loo. The bathroom is just off the lounge. I tap my feet and breathe heavily through my nose just to make some noise. I don't want to hear him pissing, this man who must make everything right.

"Y'know, the best thing you can do is to get *yourself* some support," he says, emerging from the bathroom, wiping his hands down the front of his blue jeans.

This is not what I want to hear. *I'm* fine. Gainfully employed, clean, sober and solvent, soon-to-be-homeowner, mother-to-be, fine. It's Enver, *he's* the one who needs support. I don't say any of this.

"Get yourself to some support groups." He hands me one of the dirty mugs and sits down on the two-seater next to me.

"Here's a number," he says, peering down his nose through smeary bifocals at his phone. "I'm sending it to you."

My bag buzzes and vibrates next to my foot.

"Call her. Andrea. She'll help you." I feel like my head is falling off my shoulders.

"I'm not the one who needs help!" I want to scream. "If he'd just do what I say, everything would be fine!"

We sip our rancid tea for a few minutes.

"Why do you stay with him?" he finally asks, interrupting the silence. He's not being facetious, but I bristle nonetheless.

"'Cos I love him," I say, sounding like one of those hapless women on those awful American tabloid talk shows.

He laughs. "Bloody stupid reason."

I get it. He's seen it all before.

Voiceover: *He can't stay clean longer than a few months, has difficulty holding down a job and has a history of compulsive dishonesty – ladies and gentlemen, let's welcome long-time smackhead Enver and his delusional AND PREGNANT girl-friend Sara-Jayne to the show!* *rapturous applause*

I'm embarrassed. I'm one of those women I think I hate.

"And what do you love about him?" Jimmy cocks his head, grinning.

I open my mouth, but there's nothing. I don't know who we're even talking about. The Enver from before, or this Enver.

"I … I … I love … I mean, he, *he* … um … he?"

There's a tap on the window. I look up and see Enver standing on the stoep holding one of the dusty cats. He looks like a Bond villain.

"He loves animals," I say.

Jimmy walks to the door, opens it and heads back to the sofa, perching on one of its arms. Enver just stands there in the doorway, still holding the cat.

"Well, come in then," says Jimmy. Enver does as he's told.

Ladies and gentlemen, Enver is here today to explain to Sara-Jayne why he's been MIA recently. She's worried he's headed for danger and says if he'd just do what she tells him to do, everything would be okay!

Studio audience: *Ooooooh!*

"What's going on?" I demand. "What's happening? Where have you been?" Enver's sitting across from me in an armchair in dire need of reupholstering, head bowed, looking down at the floor.

"Enver," says Jimmy. "What do you want to tell Sara-Jayne today?"

This is it, ladies and gentlemen, some big revelations are about to come from Enver on the show today.

He doesn't answer and I'm aware of the rage building between my ears.

"All I want is the truth," I tell him, which isn't true. I want him to say, "I'm sorry, everything's going to be fine. I love you, I love the baby. Everything will be okay."

"Just tell the truth!" I say again, raising my voice.

Studio audience: *Tell the truth! Tell the truth!*

"What do you want to know?" he asks quietly.

"The methadone. What happened? When did you take it?"

"I can't remember ..." He shakes his head.

"Stop dicking about, Enver. Tell her everything – she deserves that," interjects Jimmy sharply.

And so he does. And it's worse than I could ever have imagined.

8

Revelations

There's a feeling you get just before you're about to faint that is really the strangest sensation. Not unpleasant. Almost like a benzo buzz, almost like vertigo. It's physical and also out-of-body. It starts, like bubbles, in your feet and then travels into your calves, a barely perceptible hum, up through the backs of your thighs, into your spine, warming every vertebra until it taps its way into your shoulders, sneaks into your earlobes and then becomes a rhythm section of vibrations between your skull and your brain where it jams for a while until you black out.

I'm sitting in Jimmy's lounge, staring at Enver. He's talking, but I can't hear him. I can see his mouth moving, I can see Jimmy also staring intently at him, but all I can hear is a low buzz. My fingertips are tingling, and I look down to check that my hands are still attached to my body. In the space where my heart used to be is a large black balloon, which expands every time I inhale; I know that if I don't concentrate *really* hard, it will burst and I will pass out on the rug under my feet, and I don't want to do that because it's covered in cat hair.

It has *all* been a lie. Everything. *None* of it is real. Pushed by Jimmy, Enver tells me that he is in full-blown heroin addiction and has been for months; in fact, he's never really *stopped* using, not since we've been back together, not for any period of time.

For years he has just fluctuated between smoking the stuff and taking methadone and, until recently, managed to hide both from me. Things are now so bad that these days, he says, he uses just to feel normal, to stave off the clucking – the agonising body aches, the sweats and the vomiting ("It's like the worst flu you've ever had," he says). Not just that, but in recent months he has started spiking, injecting the brown liquid into his veins. At that, I feel like I might actually cease to exist, right here, on the edge of this fucking awful sofa. How is this *possible*? All is lost.

While Enver's lips move, my mind flashes back over the last couple of years, reliving certain moments like a movie montage. There we are on his birthday, smiling and celebrating, and on Valentine's Day at the cottage in the mountains, making endless love and laying underneath the stars in satiated silence. At a music concert swaying together, my back pressed against his chest, his arm protectively curled around my middle. And there we are, 11 weeks ago, at home, in bed, my head on his chest, having just conceived a baby who will arrive in our lives in 29 weeks ... Arrive to what exactly?

Was none of it real? How could I not have seen it?

Because he's an expert at hiding it.

Am I so self-absorbed that I was unable to see that the man I lived with, slept next to, allowed into my body, the love of my goddamn life, was mainlining heroin into his goddamn veins! How could I not have seen it?

Because you weren't looking for it.

Over 10 years in recovery myself and I couldn't see that he was in active addiction, right under my nose? Why didn't I see it?

You did see it – you just weren't able to believe it.

And then I start to realise and remember. Flashes of the past, arguments deliberately started so he'd have an "out" to disappear, empty medicine bottles hidden under the sink and in the toes of shoes pushed to the back of the wardrobe. The "stolen" cell phones and the missing iPad, the Abercrombie T-shirts I'd brought back from San Francisco that I never saw him wearing and that he told me were at his mom's house. His mom's house! The reason we so rarely went there, is because she knew about his using all along. Suddenly, the pennies start to drop until it sounds like a slot machine in my head.

When I'm finally able to hear again, I start to catch bits of Enver's monologue. "... wanted to tell you ... scared ... should have just been honest ... thought I could come right on my own ... kept telling myself I'd stop tomorrow ... love you ..."

All he needs is a spotlight and he'd be an actor doing an audition for a one-man play about a heroin addict telling his pregnant girlfriend he's been lying to her for years. Some time passes and I finally force myself to speak.

"What about the drug tests? They came back clean." It's almost as if *I'm* trying to convince *him* that what he's saying can't be true.

"There are ways to fake the tests," he says matter-of-factly.

What the fuck!

"How? What ways?"

He sighs and shifts in the chair, visibly reluctant to give away the trade secrets.

"What ways, Enver?" I demand.

"Tell her," says Jimmy.

"Apple juice, tea, keeping clean urine hidden in bottles around the house. Keeping it in a condom when it's time to do the test." This last one simply floors me.

"And where the fuck are you getting clean piss from, Enver?"

He doesn't answer; he just shrugs and for a second has the decency to look ashamed.

"And your job? The business?" I speak the words into the

space between us, but I'm not really asking a question; I'm simply looking for confirmation that I still exist, but even when I hear my own voice vibrating through my skull I am not relieved.

"Not true," is all he says.

There is *no* job. There is *no* business. There is no issue with his salary because there is no salary. No early commute to the office. No working late. No clean piss. No NA meetings. There is no sobriety. There is no truth. There is no happily-ever-after. There is no us. And as I look at the man hunched in a chair in front of me, his right leg jittering, I realise … There is no Enver. Not any more.

"If there's anything else you feel you need to tell her, now's the time," says Jimmy, getting up and switching the kettle on.

"That's it," Enver says. I'm struggling to take anything in.

"That's it," I repeat because I've lost all of my *own* words. I only realise I'm shaking when I feel a drop of hot tea spill onto my hands. When I look up at Enver, he's crying big black tears from his deceitful black eyes.

This. Cannot. Be. Happening.

"So, whaddaya gonna do, Enver?" asks Jimmy eventually.

Yeah, Enver, whaddaya gonna do?

"I'm gonna get clean and do meetings," he replies.

"Don't fuck about!" counters Jimmy sharply. "If you're not, don't say you are."

"I am!" promises Enver. "I can't believe I've let things get this far. I want to be in my child's life."

"Are you prepared to do whatever it takes? Recovery comes first?"

"Yes."

Whatever it takes.

Enver leaves ahead of me and, as he stands up to go, it takes everything in me not to fall at his feet and beg him to please,

please take it seriously this time. Not for me, not for us, but for the baby. Even though I know that's not how recovery works – "You've got to do it for *yourself*" – this is the last chance. I also want to beg him not to leave *me*, but I don't.

When he's gone, Jimmy stands at the sink washing our cups and asks how I'm doing. I don't know him well enough to have my breakdown on his living-room floor, so I shrug and tell him I'll be okay, even though I know I won't.

"He *can* get clean, y'know. If he wants to."

It's true. I've seen miracles happen when it comes to addicts coming right. People on the brink of life, the brink of death, who've been able to turn their lives around and rebuild the wreckage of their past. But I've also known and loved and buried people, too many people, who've simply been unable to do it. Unable, really, to get honest, which is basically what recovery is all about. Which one will Enver be?

I drive home in a state of shock. I don't have the capacity to truly connect with what's happened, so I turn up the radio until it hurts my ears. When I get to the house, I crawl into bed and pull my arms around myself.

Three days later, I have another appointment with Dr Wondimu. I am now 12 weeks pregnant, which, according to the app, means the baby is now the size of a plum. Although I haven't seen him since the horror show at Jimmy's, I've told Enver he can come with me to the hospital. The truth is, I can't bear the thought of going alone, and perhaps seeing the baby on the screen again will be enough for him to really commit and follow through with his promise to get clean. I agree to fetch him at his mother's house. We drive to the hospital in silence.

In Dr Wondimu's room I manoeuvre myself up onto the bed, just like before. Enver stands next to me. This time there is no hand-holding. I lie back and stare up at the ceiling, aware suddenly of the heat rising up the back of my neck. I hope I'm not getting sick.

"You comfortable up there, Mommy?" says Dr Wondimu, smiling his kind smile. I nod.

Mommy. I'm going to be someone's mommy.

The heat is now in my cheeks and I realise that what I'm feeling is shame. I shouldn't be up here, on this nice doctor's nice bed. I shouldn't be spoken to kindly or offered pillows to put under my knees as he's just done. I should be punished for letting things get this far. For bringing a baby into the world with a heroin addict. For being so blind and stupid and selfish that I couldn't even see what was happening right in front of me. For ignoring all the warning signs. What sort of person does that? It's basically child abuse. I'm despicable. What would Dr Wondimu think of me if he knew that's the kind of person he's looking after? I'm utterly ashamed and try to make myself and my shame smaller while still on the bed.

"How have you been feeling?" asks Wondimu, pressing some buttons on the ultrasound machine.

I nod, and manage to avoid looking over at Enver.

"Goooood," he says, pushing the ultrasound wand inside me. "Comfortable, Mommy?"

Not really, but I nod again anyway.

I can't do this. I can't be someone's mommy. Not on my own.

"And, Daddy, you're doing okay? Looking after this one?" Wondimu smiles and tilts his head in my direction.

Enver nods and says, "Mmm." I want to leap off the bed and lunge at him.

Wondimu makes a few notes in his file and then turns to us.

"Okaaaay ... So. We want to know if we're having a girl or a boy?"

"What, now? Today?"

"Yes!" Wondimu laughs. "Right now."

74

Enver and I had already agreed, in the time "before", that when it came to it, we would find out the sex of the baby. But so much has happened since then. Do we still want to know? Do we *need* to know?

"Yes," says Enver when I don't respond.

"Weeeell, by the looks of things, Mommy and Daddy, you're going to have a little girl!"

I start crying, loudly. It's not disappointment, not joy. I'm crying out of sheer relief. Boys need their fathers. I'm having a girl. There's the slightest chance that, if I'm to raise this baby alone, without Enver, I might just be enough for it. For her.

We leave Dr Wondimu's rooms and walk in silence back along the long corridor to the lift. When the doors open, I'm reflected back at myself. To infinity and beyond. Too many of me to count. Getting smaller, smaller, smaller in the mirrors. I feel like I might suffocate, so I shut my eyes. When we reach the ground floor, I practically sprint out of the lift.

"Thanks for letting me come today," says Enver as we walk to the car. I nod.

Ten minutes later, I drop him back at his mother's house and drive myself and my plum baby straight to The Clinic.

9

The Clinic

I pull into the car park, the familiarity of the place allowing me to confidently take the perilously sharp turn into the space closest to the back entrance. The telltale signs of first-time visitors are evident from the paint marks, a kaleidoscope of colours about a metre high on the corner of the wall.

I sit with the engine off for a couple of minutes before heading in, the scan of the baby, our daughter, mine and Enver's, fluttering on the dashboard. I've sat in this exact space almost a dozen times since I was first here over a decade ago. Usually, when I sit here, I am comforted because I know that whatever it is that has brought me back, I will be safe once I step inside. I will be held and soothed (and medicated) back to health by the nurse angels inside, and when I leave three weeks later, I'll definitely feel better going out than I had going in. Not this time, though. This time I doubt I'll ever feel better again. This time I wish I'd *never* been here before, because that would mean I'd never met Enver and I wouldn't be here, right now, in this unimaginable hell with his child in my belly.

I always prefer to go into The Clinic via the back entrance. For one thing, it means avoiding the inevitable eyeballing from patients sitting out front, smoking away their sorrows, tranked out of their minds. Not exactly the most uplifting welcoming party. But also, it's the familiarity of going in through the back, the absence of formality and officialdom, like going somewhere you know you're always welcome. In some ways, going in through the back door of The Clinic is like coming home.

Regardless of which way I go in, to get to the reception area I must navigate the corridors of history. The museum of me and Enver. Dragging my small suitcase behind me, I make my way through the memories. I walk past the dining room where we exchanged our first words. The stench of butternut and gem squash stewing in a bain-marie sends a wave of morning sickness over me. Even out of the corner of my eye I can see it's changed a bit since Enver and I were here 11 years ago. It's had a few facelifts, but essentially it's still the same. It's still a dining room.

At reception it's a similar story. Some superficial upgrades. A lick of paint. Polished Pebble has been replaced by Tuscany Dusk. The same but different. The guy at the desk is the same one who saw me shuffling in – thin, bandaged and bewildered – all those years ago. He's aged, obviously, and that makes me uncomfortable. It means that time has passed, and yet I haven't moved on. He smiles affably but is professional enough not to show his recognition of me as a serial offender.

I sign a few forms and even though I'd assured my doctor on the phone earlier that I'm not suicidal (and I'm not, there's a difference between wanting to be dead and actively trying to kill yourself), she's suggested that I be admitted into the High Care unit. In order to make me feel "more contained". She's fooling no one – I suspect she thinks I might get up to my old tricks again if I'm admitted into Gen Pop, and who can blame her? I don't have a great track record.

Even though I could find the security and surveillance of High Care with my eyes closed, I am led along the exact corridor where I first saw Enver and assigned a room opposite the nurse's station. It's one I've been in before. The last time was a few years back. Enver and I had been reunited for close on a year after he'd once again resurfaced in my life, full of potential and promises. The eternal Prodigal Boyfriend.

10

Love is a losing game

October 2016, Cape Town

It's 07:57am on a Monday morning and Amy Winehouse is singing into my ear.

I'm in bed, where I have every intention of staying and sleeping for at least the next four hours. Who the fuck calls this early?

Almost 8am is early to me these days, because I don't get home from work until after 2am. I've been hosting a late-night radio show in Cape Town since moving back down from Johannesburg a little over a year ago. I've relocated on the premise of being closer to my half-brother, my biological mother's son, whom I'd finally met at the age of 27, at the tail end of my rehab stay, and whom I've rather optimistically imagined is as keen on pursuing a relationship as I am. On the home front, I've been staying with Sheila, a close friend of both Enver's and mine, whom we had met in The Clinic all those lifetimes ago.

Amy's still singing.

I'm exhausted. I flew in from London late last night, having attended the wedding of a friend, the last of my university crew to tie the knot. If I'd realised in saying yes to being a bridesmaid how many "always the bridesmaid, never the bride" comments I'd have to endure, I never would have gone. It feels good to be back in my own bed.

Love, Amy reminds me, is a losing game.

I slide my hand under the pillow to retrieve my bleating phone. Squinting at the screen, I see it's a landline, a Cape Town number, vaguely familiar, but one I can't immediately place. I don't want to answer. It might be the gym. One of their friendly but simultaneously shaming courtesy calls: "Hello, Miss King, we haven't seen you for several months, so just touching base to see how you are?" Oh, hi, yeah, no I'm still fat and still too lazy to do anything about it. Thanks for calling, bye. *Ugh*. No thanks. On the other hand, what if someone's died? Or been in a car accident? Or died in a car accident? Catastrophising is my default. I quickly swipe my thumb over the screen, silencing Amy mid-chorus.

"Hello?" I say guardedly.

"Sara-Jayne." It's a statement, not an enquiry, and whoever's on the other end is smiling as they say my name. The voice is familiar, but I can't place it right away.

"Yes, who is this?"

"How are you?" grins the voice.

"Fine. Who *is* this?" I snap.

A chuckle through the handset.

It can't be.

"Who is this?" I ask again, rearranging myself on the bed as if The Voice might at any minute walk in through the door and catch me in my nightdress and headscarf.

Another laugh. Deep, sexy.

It is. It's him.

"Who do you think it is?"

Never a straight answer with this one, always answering a question with a question, but I'm the one smiling now.

"Enver," I confirm, sitting up against the headboard and reaching for a lighter and cigarette. Even after everything, I still love how his name sounds in my mouth.

Another chuckle.

"How are you, Sara-Jayne?"

He always does this, this faux formality as if we haven't tasted the rawness of each other on our tongues and trembled breathlessly into each other's hair a hundred times over.

"I'm fine, Enver, and how are you?" I reply, mimicking his stiff tone.

I'm sitting completely upright now, back against the headboard, legs crossed. Cigarettes and lighter in my lap. I light one and inhale contentedly.

"That's good," he says. "I'm glad you're doing well." He doesn't answer my how-are-you.

"Did you get my postcard?" I ask.

Over the years, I've sent Enver postcards from all over. Florence, Cyprus, Paris, Marrakech, Kuala Lumpur and, most recently, London. The message is always a variation of the same. *Hope you're well.* I've always just wanted him to be okay and for him to know that even if he's not, somewhere out there there's someone who's thinking about him. Addiction is lonely as hell.

"No, I didn't get a postcard," he tells me. "So, how are you Sara-Jayne? What can you tell me?"

He always does this too. Deflects attention away from himself. It's not a good sign.

Three years have passed since I packed up my life in London and returned to South Africa so Enver and I could pick up where we'd left off and finally start living the life we'd once planned. But, if God laughs when we make plans, then addiction is rendered positively hysterical, and things hadn't come to pass in the way I'd thought they would. Not at all.

As soon as I'd arrived in Cape Town, I realised it would no longer be possible to keep ignoring the red flags I'd been determinedly overlooking for the past few months. In the weeks leading up to me leaving London, Enver's behaviour had become increasingly erratic. He'd be uncontactable for days on end and then offer unlikely excuses when I eventually managed to get hold of him. I was suspicious, but my suspicions were no match for my denial or my desire to get back onto the path of our happily-ever-after. The feelings I had for Enver had returned so quickly and intensely when he reappeared that I couldn't bring myself to admit the *thing* that stood between us and our happy ending.

His disappearing act had continued when I got to Cape Town, but eventually I tracked him down to his parents' house, by which time it was impossible to keep denying what was going on.

"Enver, what is happening? I've been trying to get hold of you for a week. Please just be honest with me," I'd pleaded on the phone.

"I never meant for things to be like this."

"Like *what*, Enver? Where have you been?"

"I've been at home," he said quietly. We both knew he didn't mean his parents' house. His promises to end things with her, the woman he'd been living with for the last couple of years, had been constant throughout the months of our reconnection. Constant but unactioned.

As a means of self-preservation, I'd decided early on not to ask him about her in case what I discovered shattered the version of *us* I'd started to conjure in my head. And yet I'd been unable to stop myself from seeking out everything I could about her. I discovered where they lived, where she worked, how many siblings she had. I saw that, like me, she was a fan of Whitney Houston and, very much unlike me, loved reality TV. I also saw that she and Enver had spent the Easter before last at the beach. One photo showed them on the sand, squinting into the sun at the camera. I had dozens of similar pictures of Enver and me. Because it made me feel better, I'd decided that she wasn't his type. Too homely. There was a lot I told myself, untruths that made me feel better. Unlike Enver and his girlfriend, my denial and self-preservation were a match made in heaven.

"Enver. What's going on?" I'd begged.

Silence.

"Enver!"

He didn't answer, but I heard him loud and clear.

The unsaid had already been said many times over the last few months, but I'd had my hands over my ears.

"Let's meet for coffee," I suggested. If I could just *see* him, I thought, face to face, then I could make him see. Make him see that it's *possible*. Life, love, all of it without drugs. Nearly six years in recovery and still I believed I could love the addiction out of him.

I convinced him to meet me at the train station in town. While I walked, shaking, along the platform to the turnstile, I wondered whether I would even recognise him. But then, there he was … and of course I did. He looked the same. Still take-my-breath-away beautiful. Everything still the same. Except his eyes. They betrayed the lie his smile was trying to tell the world. I pulled him into a hug, shocked at how my body reacted to being so close to him again.

We found a coffee spot close by. He sat across from me, and I stretched my hands across the table, just further than the mid-point between us. An invitation; I wanted so badly for him to reach out, but he didn't. I wanted him to open up, or break down, but he didn't. I wanted him to tell me he loved me. He didn't.

Instead, we talked and laughed and cautiously reminisced about the good times. The good old days. There were moments when it seemed impossible that six whole years had gone by since we were last so close to one another. Within touching distance. There were moments too when, watching his hands and his mouth, I was suddenly visited by flashbacks of his lips on the softest part of me, his fingers moving inside me. Snapshots of a past long gone.

We didn't talk about what had happened over the last few months. We chose to ignore the lies he'd told and the promises he'd made. We pretended that we'd never spoken about marriage or the children we would have and we certainly didn't mention the fact that I'd just left my entire life in London to come back and start a new one with him.

We managed to eke out two coffees and the rest of my Marlboros over two hours that raced by all too quickly. I'd been about to order us two more Americanos when Enver said he had to go. I tried my best to mask my disappointment.

"Unless ..." he said.

"Unless, what?"

"Unless ... you want to wait."

For?

"For?"

"F-For me to sort myself out."

I didn't know what he meant initially, although I noticed he'd started to become slightly agitated. I didn't realise it was the junk eking itself out of his system, bringing intolerable reality in through a crack, bit by agonising bit. The fact that, to me, Enver still didn't *look* like a heroin addict made it even harder for me to fully grasp just how bad his using had become.

"I have to sort myself out," he said again, managing to sound matter-of-fact and apologetic at the same time. Eventually, I realised he meant he had to go and take a hit.

I didn't have many boundaries (as I'd been told by a succession of therapists and sponsors in recent years) but I knew *this* was definitely one of them. I couldn't sit there watching balding, one-legged pigeons pecking at cigarette butts and dry chewing gum on the concrete while Enver went off to chase the dragon.

"I should be going anyway," I lied. But the truth was I'd have sat there with him until Doomsday if he didn't have to go. He walked with me back to the station.

"SJ," he said as I rummaged in my bag for my train ticket, "I hate to ask but can you maybe help me out with some money, for a train ticket, like R25?"

A ticket was R10.

I looked up at him. Why did he have to do that?

"I … I can't, Enver."

"That's okay, I understand. It was nice to see you, Sara-Jayne."

I could see he hated himself for asking. I hated him a little too.

"It was nice to see *you*, Enver."

I was about to walk away when he said, "I'm sorry. I'm sorry you had to see me like this." He'd dropped his guard and looked thoroughly ashamed.

"Stop it," I told him. "This is *me*. I just want you to be okay." And it was true. I did. Back then, I just wanted him to be okay. Even if it meant we couldn't be together. Even if it meant he would never leave Easter Beach Girl. Even if it meant shattering my heart into a million little pieces again.

Don't look back, don't look back, don't look back, I told myself after we'd hugged goodbye and I was walking to the train. I looked back. Enver was already skarreling, weaving between unsuspecting rush-hour commuters. Flashing them that killer smile. I kept looking long enough to see a petite blonde laughing up at him, reaching into her handbag and handing him a R20 note.

On the train, I pulled out my phone and saw that I had several missed calls. All of them from the same Joburg number. I called back. It was the editor at a TV station where I'd had a job interview a few days before, when I'd first got back to Cape Town.

"If you're still interested, Sara-Jayne, we'd like to offer you the job."

"I'm definitely interested," I replied.

"Great, great! The only thing is, we've had to move the role from Cape Town to our Joburg offices. Is that going to be a problem?"

I looked out at the mountain doing its best to hide beneath its cloudy tablecloth, and I knew I couldn't stay in Cape Town. I had to put some distance between me and this unpredictability I'd allowed back into my life. There was no way I was going back to England, but I also couldn't spend my life willing Enver to get his shit together. I also didn't relish the thought of potentially running into him (and her) every time I popped out for a pint of milk and a pack of smokes. I had to leave. Again.

"Joburg?" I say. "No, that won't be a problem at all."

Two weeks later, my broken heart and I packed up once again and flew to Johannesburg, where I would spend nearly three years doing my best (with varying degrees of success) not to think about Enver.

Even though this early-morning phone call has come out of the blue and I'm still trying to get my post-flight bearings, I am not caught entirely unawares because there's always a part of me that is Enver-ready. Ready to drop everything to get back on the merry-go-round that is us. I know how it looks to the outside world. Desperate, naive, pitiful, stupid, completely fucking mad; I tell myself it's love. Fate. There's nothing that could ever happen, no amount of time passing, that could change the way I see Enver. Even after everything that's happened.

I'd seen him three, maybe four times after I moved to Joburg. Whenever I visited Cape Town, I'd reach out. "I'm in the area – fancy a coffee?" I never let on that I always orchestrated a way to be "in the area".

We'd go for long drives in my car, always him at the wheel and me fighting the urge to put my hand on his knee. We'd find somewhere to have a coffee or a Coke, which would inevitably turn into lunch, sometimes supper. On one occasion, we ended up in bed, but it had been awkward and, unusually, not terribly satisfying. I think I still reeked of wanting more from him than he knew he was able to give, and his inability to tell me the truth about how bad his using had become meant that achieving any real level of intimacy was essentially impossible.

Self-protection forced me to convince myself that these occasional rendezvous were nothing more than two old friends catching up and shooting the shit, but it was more than that. I knew all too well that addiction was progressive. If he didn't commit to getting off the smack, his fate was sealed. "Jails, institutions and death" – that's what we said in the meetings. I *needed* to see Enver, to make sure that he was okay. And, if I was being honest, to see if I could still feel the spark that might signal that one day there could still be the possibility of us.

My love life while I'd been in Joburg had been fairly uneventful. A few insignificant Tinder flings and one relatively brief but semi-serious relationship. I'd really cared for the guy – a kind, older, dependable Australian – but the Ghost of Boyfriend Past simply refused to be exorcised. Sometimes while I lay in the Australian's arms, safe and sated, I'd wonder what might happen if Enver turned up one day, clean and sober and professing his love. The answer was always the same, and it always left me feeling slightly unsettled.

"So you didn't get my postcard then?" I'm now wide awake, pulled back into the right time zone thanks to Enver's call.

"No postcard. How's life treating you?"

"Great!" Not strictly true, because I'm two months out of The Clinic after a crippling bout of depression, but I don't want to talk about that.

We make small talk for a couple of minutes and then we return to our familiar script. "I've got an appointment at the doctor later [I haven't], so I'll be in the area. Fancy a coffee?" I do my best to sound breezy. He seems to buy it and 90 minutes later I'm outside his parents' house. It takes exactly one afternoon for Enver and I to get back on the merry-go-round.

We take a drive to watch the boats at the harbour. We eat fish and chips. We walk shoulder to shoulder along the beach and we smoke, passing cigarettes back and forth between our lips like we used to do. It's music to my ears when he tells me he's no longer with Easter Beach Girl. He seems remorseful that he's hurt her, but relieved to be out of a relationship he says he was in for the wrong reasons. He admits his using had taken its toll on her and that eventually she'd had enough. "I wasn't man enough to leave when I should have," he admits. I'm grateful for his honesty.

In the evening he drives me back to Sheila's. "Let's have supper here and then I'll drop you home?" I suggest, avoiding looking him in the eye. We both know he's going to spend the night. And he does. And the next night and the night after that and the night after that.

Because we're not people of moderation, Enver and I dive, headfirst, back into one another, deep and in over our heads. I don't think to question what we're doing because, in my mind, love is the answer. Enver is the answer. He's also the reward. Enver is my reward for getting myself together, for staying clean, for waiting it out. For staying when I could have left, for leaving when I could have stayed, for enduring the bad men, the sad men, the you're-completely-fucking-mad men, and the just-don't-tell-my-wife men. Enver is what I get for remembering the fundamental crux of all those books I read during my childhood.

Love. Is. All. You. Need. Enver, the only one I ever needed. Enver is the prize, the universe's gift to me. "Here," it seems to be saying, "*now* you're ready … You've earned this." I genuinely believe we are meant to be together.

I also believe that the entirely unsuitable Tinder acquisition I've been stepping out (and staying in) with for the past couple of months should be happy for me when I call and tell him that the love of my life has returned and that this, whatever you want to call what we've been doing, has now come to an end. Thank-you-good-luck-goodbye-but-I'm-in-love-with-someone-else-no-hard-feelings-but-really-you-must-have-known-this-was-never-going-to-work-and-it's-not-you-it's-me-I-mean-it's-you-too-obviously-but-mostly-it's-*him*-because-did-I-mention-he's-the-love-of-my-life-and-so-thanks-for-the-handful-of-orgasms-you-helped-me-have-even-though-honestly-I-was-thinking-about-him-the-whole-time-so-sorry-but-so-long-farewell-bye-bye-see-ya-later-peace-out.

A couple of days into our reunion honeymoon I ask Enver if we can talk. It's time to address the dragon in the room.

"I love you," I tell him. "I've always loved you, but this isn't going to work if you're not clean. *Properly* clean. From everything."

Enver – who, on the face of it, is still showing no obvious signs of being a junkie – has been upfront about the fact he's using methadone. It allows him, for the most part, to pass himself off as a normal, functional member of society, but it doesn't help with the underlying reasons *why* he uses in the first place. At nearly 10 years in recovery, my definition of what it means to be clean is unwavering and it certainly doesn't include synthetic drug substitutes.

"I want to be with someone who's healthy in their body *and* their mind, Enver. Using methadone is just masking the feelings that make you want to use in the first place." There's a brief silence. "I love you," I tell him again, "but this is a non-negotiable for me. You need to stop the methadone and do meetings if we're really going to give this another go."

It's not an easy conversation and it's a gamble, because it's what Enver and I have butted heads over for years. He thinks the heroin is the cause; I think it's the effect. But his response leaves me even more convinced that we're on the path of destiny, and he agrees to come clean, properly, and do what needs to be done for his recovery. "I'll support you 100%, whatever you need," I tell him and I mean it. Later that day we get everything together that he needs to see him through a gruelling five-day cold turkey in my bedroom at Sheila's.

Thinking I'm helping, I tell Enver that I'm happy to take care of things financially for a while so that he can focus on staying clean and, for the first few months, things are okay. I'm reminded that Enver is one of the kindest people I know. He drives me to and from work every night, cooks for me and checks the oil and water in my car. He rubs my feet without protest and strokes my hair until I fall asleep on his chest. He slow dances with me on the cold kitchen tiles and can snap me out of a bad mood in an instant by twirling me in a pirouette without warning. This is what I think constitutes a good relationship.

But what I haven't left any room for is the effect of nearly 15 years of heroin addiction. Enver was a teenager when he began using and it's left him in a time warp. Emotionally, he's hovering somewhere between childhood and adolescence. He can be petulant and puerile and sometimes I can scarcely believe I'm having such nonsensical arguments with a 33-year-old.

Meanwhile, I'm still chasing my own impossible high. I'm naively trying to recreate the early days of our relationship but doggedly ignoring everything that's happened in the years in between. I want the Enver from back then, but I also want him to be at the same place as I am, not nearly a decade behind, playing developmental catch-up.

In the end, even though I've managed to stay on top of my sobriety since going to rehab, I know nothing about dealing with another person in early recovery and, mentally and emotionally, I'm completely out of my depth.

Ten months after Enver and I get back together, and two weeks before I'm due to publish a book, I'm forced to check myself back into The Clinic.

Enver comes to see me every day. At 6pm, almost on the dot, he arrives, tapping on the glass with his long, tobacco-stained fingers to alert the nurses that he's there.

I lean into him when he hugs me, determined to take some kind of comfort from his presence. I'm still years away from checking his pupils, or pulling my nostrils in to see, without him noticing, if I can detect that faint but telltale sign that he's been using. Cheating on me with Mistress H. Every day he stays well past the end of visiting hours because the nurses love him and remind me, often, how lucky I am to have someone who clearly loves me so much and would do anything for me. "Especially with all of this," says one of the older nursing sisters, making a sweeping motion indicating the buff-coloured walls of High Care. So lucky. They don't know, and neither do I, that before arriving every day, Enver takes a detour to his dealer, so that by the time he comes to see me he's appropriately medicated against his very own "all of this".

11

Don't be like Pat

I watched a TV show once about an American free diver who could drop her heart rate to 11 beats a minute. The deeper she went, the smaller her lungs became, forcing her heart to beat slower. At its slowest, it was the same as that of a whale, the presenter had said. She could also stay underwater for four minutes without breathing. The risk to the brain and the heart was extreme.

If I could, I'd stop my heart from beating, I think as I sit perched on the end of the bed in High Care. I haven't moved since I got here an hour ago. I've just been sitting. Still. My breath so shallow I don't even see the rise of my chest when I inhale. Outward displays of "alive" are simply too much for me right now.

My small, granite-coloured suitcase is still parked just behind the door, exactly where I left it when I arrived. Every 10 minutes one of the nurses comes in, presumably to check if I'm swinging from the light fixture, and the back of the door crashes against it. But still I don't move.

I'm waiting for my doctor. I'm told she's doing her rounds and I'm her last patient before lunch. Dr Dolly has been my psychiatrist for a while now. She's the fifth shrink I've had since being diagnosed as officially mad nearly 12 years ago and she's easily my favourite. Perhaps because she's a little cuckoo herself and doesn't try to hide it. She's saved my life several times. She also has the most ridiculous name I've ever heard for a doctor.

Shrinks have been a regular and essential part of my life since the first time I sat on a psychiatrist's couch at the age of 27. I'd been in rehab a little over a week when it was suggested by one of the counsellors that I might benefit from a psychiatric evaluation and possibly even a prescription for medication. I was instantly offended, horrified by the suggestion, and nearly repacked the baggage (actual and metaphorical) I'd barely begun to unload since arriving. Things were starting to feel a little too *Girl, Interrupted* for my liking.

Despite my struggles, I knew very little about mental health and my frame of reference when it came to psychiatric diagnoses and treatment was embarrassingly narrow. In my mind, it was one thing to have some counselling sessions with a kindly looking hippy in an Aran sweater, but another thing entirely to need actual psychiatric treatment. I had an idea of the type of people who needed to see shrinks and take head meds and be admitted to actual psychiatric wards. They were not people like me. They were people like my mum's friend Pat, a woman she'd met in the late sixties when they'd lived in the same digs in London.

I'd never met Pat, but she existed throughout my childhood and adolescence as an icon for the mad and bewildered. Every so often a letter would arrive bearing a familiar scrawl. "It's from Pat," my mum would say, her voice laden with pity. Pat's name had to be said softly, and sadly. When one spoke about her, one needed to do so solemnly. A mysterious, woeful creature, Pat was afflicted in ways never directly verbalised, yet I understood who she was and what she represented. Pat was always in The Clinic and whenever I thought of her sitting down to write her shaky, scribbled letters in black ink, I imagined a wretched, hand-wringing creature, benzoed up to her eyeballs, on the floor of her sparsely furnished "cell". In my mind, she wrote her letters with a pen she would have to return, to a nurse or orderly as soon as she was done, lest her madness take hold and she plunge it into her hand or eye or heart. Pat, as far as I could understand, was a grown-up who needed to be treated like a child.

To me, the beginning, middle and end of Pat was a mad, faceless figure who appeared in our lives by way of these occasional letters. I never thought of her as being anything apart from "Mum's mad friend". No one ever sat me down to talk about who Pat was outside her mental-health struggles. In fact, there was never *any* discussion about Pat, and what I took away from that was that if you were "mental", that's all you were, and that it was definitely better *not* to be mental. The other thing I took away from it all was *shame*. Being mad, being sad and definitely being admitted to a psychiatric facility was shameful.

There was also my mother's cousin, Annie, whose name too was whispered in hushed tones and who had struggled with anorexia. Again, no one talked about it directly, but as a child I managed to piece together bits of cryptic conversations heard down the curly phone line and in doorways at Christmastime. Annie was "troubled" and could be "difficult". Her own suffering meant other people suffered and that too was shameful. "*Her poor parents!*" Annie was spoken about in the same way women with PTSD or depression were spoken about in the 1800s. They may as well have said she had hysteria. Like Pat, Cousin Annie *was* her illness and that was all.

For a long time, I thought people like Pat and Annie chose to be "mad" and "difficult", in the same ignorant way people think all fat people choose to be overweight or drug addicts choose to stick needles in themselves.

I didn't want to go to a psychiatrist, and I didn't want to be mad and, if I was, I especially didn't want anyone else to know about it. I remember being absolutely, illogically terrified that someone might see me visiting a shrink. It was bad enough that I was in rehab (even the Lindsay Lohan/Amy Winehouse rehab chic gaining traction at the time wasn't enough to completely remove the shame of that), but what if I was actually *diagnosed* with something? That would be the final straw. Law graduates from Surrey who'd gone to Pony Club didn't go for psychiatric evaluations. We hitched up our big-girl riding breeches, pouted our stiff upper lips and didn't make much ado about nothing.

An appointment was made for me to see a psychiatrist at a clinic about 10 kilometres from the rehab. One of the assistant counsellors, also an addict in recovery and a former patient, had driven me there in the Z3 her rich lawyer daddy had bought her for managing to get to six months clean and sober. She might have been clean, but she was still bat-shit crazy.

"I'll wait in the car," she said as we pulled up to an impressive Georgian-style property. The car park was almost full, I noted.

"My appointment is after yours, so when you come out I'll go in."

"It's like the blind leading the fucking blind," I grumbled under my breath, hauling myself awkwardly out of the leather bucket seats and heading towards the automatic doors.

I felt like I was in a made-for-TV movie or part of an over-exaggerated tableau set up to depict a person visiting a psychiatrist's office for the first time. Just like poor Pat, I too was about to discover that I was almost certainly mad and it was about to be made official.

The writing was pretty much on the wall already, but I was about to pay someone, a Dr – I looked at the name scrawled on the torn-off piece of a Marlboro packet – A Sevcik an inordinate amount of money to confirm the same. Given the amount I was paying him, it was probably *his* impossibly shiny, selenite-grey S-Class taking up *two* reserved parking spaces outside, I thought.

The waiting area was a complete cliché. Unimaginative pseudo-art hanging on the beige walls, a dusty ficus leaning idly in a pot by the door and a couple of sad-looking leaflets about depression and anxiety wilting in a Perspex bookshelf above a half-empty water cooler. There was an enormous cherrywood desk behind which sat a woman who, it was clear, was deeply dissatisfied with her life. She couldn't say she was deeply dissatisfied with her life, of course, so instead she spewed little bits of her own personal misery onto the poor unfortunates like me who walked through the doors every day. She sighed loudly when I asked to borrow a pen to fill in the forms she'd given me when I arrived, unable to hide her disappointment in me.

For several minutes I sat crossing and uncrossing my legs and squinting at the ficus, unable to tell whether it was real or not. I wanted to reach out and touch its waxy green leaves so that I knew for sure, but I didn't want to get caught by the old cunt behind the cherrywood.

Eventually, I became aware of a hand being thrust towards me.

"Hello, Sah-rrrah."

I looked up and past the hand. It belonged to a tall, handsome woman with a significant nose, considerable bosom and the most atrocious dress sense. She wore a teal mohair cardigan over a plaid shirt with the collar up. Oversized tortoiseshell glasses hung on an ornate chain around her neck. A thick black leather belt into which several hundred intricately patterned holes had been pressed was doing its utmost to snatch her in at the waist and simultaneously hold up a pair of tawny brown linen culottes. She was smiling. She had coral lipstick on her bright, white teeth.

"Is so naahce to meed chew, Sah-rrrah." She trilled the R in my name as if speaking it through a flute. "Hauw arrre choo to-day?"

I didn't respond because although she was looking directly at me and calling me by my name, I still wasn't entirely sure she was talking to me.

She smiled through the silence. I was confused.

'Sah-rrrah Jayn-nee?" She either hadn't seen or had misunderstood the hyphen. She thinks Jayne is my surname, I grumbled silently to myself. There was absolutely nothing in me that had the inclination to correct her. Who the fuck is this, I thought.

"Ay yam Dok-torrr Sev-chick," she announced, reading my mind.

"Choo can call me Adrrrriana."

Dr A Sevcik. A woman, I almost said out loud. I was also struggling to place the accent. "Eastern Bloc", my late grandmother would have simplified. I'd hazard a more geographically refined guess at Lithuania or Slovakia. Czechoslovakia? No, that no longer exists, split itself in two trying to please everyone, I reminded myself.

"We go?" suggested Dr Sevcik as I got to my feet, still trying to work out up from down.

"Is this way," she beamed, reaching across and whipping a brown folder out of the gnarly grey hands of Desk Bitch. I followed her large, swinging behind as she began to stride down a corridor.

Dr Sevcik was unlike any doctor I'd ever met before. For a start, as soon as we entered her office, she kicked off across the room a pair of gaudy but not garish clog-style shoes, which then lay strewn but ornamental on the floor next to a very large Louis Vuitton tote bag. Then she planted her large brown bum in a large brown chair behind her desk and, more deftly than I had believed possible for a woman of her size, placed one enormous but immaculately painted foot on her opposite knee.

Sevcik's office, like everything about her, was large. Her desk was enormous and stretched almost the length of an entire wall.

On it was a Jenga tower of books so precariously balanced I nearly offered to relocate them to a safer locale for my own peace of mind. On the far side of the room, floor-to-ceiling French doors looked out onto a small courtyard where a black man in blue overalls tended considerately to a shocking-pink clematis. The walls were painted a light mustardy green, a colour that shouldn't have worked but did somehow. Behind her desk was a painting of a Roman amphitheatre and at the bottom the word *Pula*. On a shelf on the opposite wall, a framed certificate from the University of Zagreb, School of Medicine. Croatia. She's come a long way, I thought, and wondered what it would be like to live there.

Unsure of myself and what I should do, I stood on one foot as Sevcik bashed away at a keyboard I could see was littered with crumbs. Eventually I pulled out the chair in front of her desk, but she clapped her hands together, pirouetted in her own seat and then planted her stockinged feet on the floor before leaping up and shouting, "No!" Then she'd ushered me, like an enthusiastic waitress, over to two khaki velvet armchairs on either side of the French doors. Before allowing me to take a seat, she wrestled with them dramatically, manoeuvring them so that the left arm of one and the right arm of the other were touching.

"Seet!" she commanded, tapping one of the chairs, and, while I was trying to work out whether she was indicating the function of the piece of furniture or giving an instruction, she collapsed theatrically into the other, crossing her long legs at the ankles and leaning in close to me.

"Now, Sarrrah," she said kindly. "Choo arre not fine, yes?"

I gulped and shook my head no. Not fine. Not fine at all.

She had a clipboard balanced on her knee, two brand-new sheets of light green paper, the colour of medical scrubs, clipped to it. She stared at me and reached up into the chaos of her bottle-reddened hair (it had probably read Daring Cherry or Bright Copper Kettle on the bottle) and, like an eccentric, Croatian Mary Poppins, retrieved a Spider-Man pen, which she clicked twice to release a ballpoint tip. "My son's," she said by way of explanation, waving it at me. I was surprised. Hadn't pictured any children. A husband, maybe an overfed Shar-Pei (I wouldn't have been surprised if there was one dozing under the desk), but not a son.

"So," she said, "not fine." And scribbled something on the clipboard. "Sarrah, tell me hauw choo fil."

It was a tough one. It'd been so long since I had truly been in touch with my feelings in their truest form that I'd forgotten their names. Unable to bear yet another long silence, I gave her an answer.

"Depressed," I said, going for simplification over conversation.

"Off cowse," she nodded, returning to the clipboard.

As she wrote, I found myself staring at her hair. She'd tried, half-heartedly it seemed, to fashion it into an up-do. The result was a messy topknot. In addition to the Spider-Man pen, the hair was home to several barrettes, strewn non-committedly about, and a hairpin or two pretending to be in the business of securing some of the more flyaway wisps at the nape of her thick neck. One had abandoned its post altogether and hung down behind her ear. Her entire look was don't-give-a-shit chic. I both envied and admired it.

Sevcik looked up again. Sighed and smiled.

"And, so, choo are sad," she stated, hugging her notes to her chest.

A lump of something I thought might be truth but wasn't yet able to recognise as grief crept into my throat. I tried to swallow it down before it choked me. I was also doing my damnedest to stop the disloyal tears that had gathered in the corners of my eyes and that so desperately wanted to fall. In the end, I let them.

"Jyeeess," she said matter-of-factly, confirming her own statement. "Choo are sad."

I managed a nod.

"But *why*, Sarrah?" She hit the clipboard on her knee. "Choo are young, choo are beautiful, hmmm?"

I tried out of sheer politeness to muster a smile. I wished she hadn't said that. It made me feel worse. Like I just needed to pull myself up by the bootstraps. It felt like she'd just negated every bad feeling I'd ever had, every hurt, every tear, every loss, based on my not being ugly or old.

Young and beautiful (neither of which I felt) are the tonic for all ills, it seemed. So simple. Just like that song. The one that says, if you want to be loved, you must "keep young and beautiful". And I do, I do so desperately want to be loved, I wept inwardly.

"So," she continued, "choo are sad. Thees eees no good. Vee vant choo to be happy, yes?"

When she said "happy" she bounced the clipboard from one knee to another, rocking her head from side to side as if to remind me what happy looks like. She looked demented.

I smiled again, but this time I meant it. I was fucking miserable, but Dr Sevcik was funny. Her voice was like listening to a curious orchestra. Mostly low and long and like a cello. But when she laughed, the sound reverberated around her large, bouncy, mohair-clad chest like a rumbling bass drum. Even her sneezing was musical. Listening to her was like trying to follow a complicated concerto. As she braced for the crescentic *Ah-choo!* her nose wrinkled into itself, and her overly mascaraed eyelashes twitched like manic spiders. It happened six or seven times in a row. By the third stanza I'd begun tapping my foot on the off beat.

"Sarrah, in your family, everyone eees okay, yes?"

I didn't know what she meant. "Okay how?" I asked.

"No one ees having the mental illness, your mah-ter, your vater?"

Which family? Which mother and father? Are any of them sane? I couldn't answer her honestly. Yet another reason I *hate* being adopted. I don't even know what might lurk in my own body, I fumed silently.

"I don't know, sorry."

Sevcik nodded, mistaking my ignorance for confusion.

"I'm adopted," I added, by way of explanation, but she was already moving on.

"Sarrah, you haff job?"

"I was fired last month."

"You haff husbint, boyfriend?"

"Boyfriend, in England. He's breaking up with me."

"You haff family? Your mah-ter, she loves you?"

"I don't know," I answered truthfully.

"Sarrah, you hurt yourself sometimes?"

"Sometimes," I nodded. She did too.

"But you nevair try to tek your own laaf, Sarrah?"

Shamefully, I nodded again and Dr Sevcik shook her head. She looked genuinely sad.

"You don't luff yourself, Sarrrah." I couldn't work out if that was a statement or a question.

"Dr Sevcik," I said, "I have absolutely no idea who I am. There are some days when I wake up and can pretend to be my own best friend, and then there are other days when it's all I can do not to pour bleach down my neck and slit my fucking throat." She nodded sadly again and scribbled something on a piece of paper.

I left Sevcik's office with a prescription for Prozac and a diagnosis of bipolar.

But that was 10 years ago.

If nothing changes, nothing changes. I read out loud a sticker I'd picked up at a recovery conference in London a few years ago and which has, since then, lived affixed to my suitcase.

There's a knock on the door and Dr Dolly and her toffee-blonde bob swing into the room. I've been doing an impressive job holding it together, but I dissolve as soon as she smiles her kindly smile and pulls a chair up to the side of the bed.

"This can't be happening," I sob. "I can't do this!"

I relay the drama of the last few weeks – and she listens, as always, with just the right amount of furrows in her brow and kindness in her eyes.

"I'm a bad mother," I bawl. "I haven't even had a baby yet and I'm a bad mother." We both sit until I'm all cried out. Neither of us says anything for nearly 10 minutes. The silence is both torturous and divine.

"What can we do to *help* you, Sara-Jayne?" asks Dr Dolly gently.

I blink and look out the window into the garden. Proteas and hadedas.

"There are things we can give you to help, things that won't hurt the baby. It's crucial that we keep you contained."

She folds her hands in her lap; I notice hers are not shaking, unlike mine. I glance down at my fingernails. Ten well-manicured tips. When did my own hands start to betray me, I wonder. They tell too much. I turn them over in my lap and stare at my life line. Too long. I make fists and pull them inside the arms of my cardigan lest they remind me of even more of my failures. We've sat like this many times before, Dr Dolly and I, but never with a baby growing inside me.

A truck passes by outside, inexplicably sounding its horn loudly. I wonder what it would feel like to be crushed underneath its enormous wheels. Would my head explode like a watermelon, spilling my fleshy, scarlet brains all over the tarmac?

"What's going on for you right now? What do you need?"

Get me away from here, I'm dying, I say without moving my lips.

The truck sounds its horn again. The hadeda doesn't flinch. Desensitised. I know how it feels. Dolly inhales and then sighs contemplatively.

"I think it would be a good idea if Enver doesn't come to see you. I think you need some distance." I start crying again.

She's trying to help me, but she doesn't understand. Distance is impossible because Enver is indelible. His ink blood, the blood that runs deep dark, black tar, tar black in his veins, now also pulses fiercely through mine. Enver *has* to be here. He *has* to stop using. He *has* to, because I cannot do this on my own.

12

A mother's love

"You can open your eyes."

I'm at the family-planning clinic. I'm 16 and I'm pregnant. Maybe. I believe there is a reasonably strong possibility that I could be because I've had sex. Actual sex. The full kind.

It's been five minutes since I hovered inelegantly above the toilet bowl, knickers around my ankles, hand thrust between my legs. It's been three minutes since I handed an austere-looking NHS nurse a warm pot of my piss and waited, with (ironically) crossed legs, to check whether in my brief (very, very brief) and largely forgettable first-time fumble I've ruined my life.

After years of being the Ugly Duckling to my older brother's gorgeous Black Swan, I've inexplicably blossomed into something desired and desirable. I've also managed to acquire myself a sweet-natured but irritatingly doting Nigerian boyfriend, Ebi. Hence the sex.

It's thanks to Ebi, my absolute disregard for myself and my body and my willingness to *do* absolutely anything and *be* absolutely anybody for "love" that I've finally managed to cast off the painfully uncool shackles of a burdensome virginity. It'd really become an albatross around my cunt. Weighing me down and impeding my efforts to clamber, even by one precious, precarious rung, up the ladder of teenage social standing. When you're 16 and trying to ingratiate yourself with the popular girls, hymens are *so* last season.

I'm thankfully not stupid enough to have believed the idiotic chatter circulated around school about not getting pregnant "on your first time", but I'm also not smart enough to have stolen more than one condom from my brother's sock drawer, and we'd done it twice that afternoon. Mum had been in court all day and would be back late. Ebi and I had left college early, both feigning sickness, and caught the train back to my house, holding hands the whole way.

It hadn't been bad. Granted, it hadn't been great either. There was no blood, as some of the girls at school (and three Jilly Cooper novels) had suggested there might be. That had been a relief. It wasn't terribly painful either. I'd just felt … full. I'd made sure I'd made all the right noises and said all the right things. I'd talked about things being wet and tight and said "cock" quite a bit too. It seemed to do the trick. The last thing I wanted was for him to think during my first time that it was my first time.

I like Ebi. I do, but as he'd entered me, I'd immediately closed my eyes and started humming the theme tune from *Poirot* in my head. It was only when I couldn't remember how it ended that I realised he'd stopped moving.

"You can open your eyes."

He'd pulled out and I felt empty again.

"You can open your eyes …"

"Sara-Jayne, you can open your eyes!"

I do and I see the nurse peering at me from behind her disapproving brow.

"Well, I imagine that comes as a huge relief," she says, her cat's-bum mouth pursed into nothingness.

"What? I … I mean, pardon?" I say apologetically. I'm sorry, for her and me.

"The test is negative – you are not pregnant," she sighs and pointedly peels off the disposable latex gloves.

"I suggest you take some of these." She hands me two packets of government-issue condoms. "They're free," she adds. "I also suggest you tell all your sexual partners to wear one during intercourse."

All? Partners, plural?

Thanking her profusely, I shove them into the front pocket of my bag (where they will later be discovered by my mother) and leave, back through the waiting room. There I see Sandra Jones from my old high school, sitting in the corner, reading a leaflet and looking worried. I put my head down and scuttle out before she spots me.

In bed later that night, I place my hand over my mercifully still-uninhabited womb and thank my lucky stars. Sex is all right, I think, but the last thing I'd ever, *ever* want to be is a single mother.

For years, I rejected outright the idea that I might one day have children. There were a few reasons. One – the one I offered when people asked – was that I didn't much care for them. I didn't relish years spent in their company, wiping eternally runny noses or dealing with the daily rigmarole of the school run, wet weekends spent shivering at the edge of muddy soccer fields or regularly having salt-and-vinegar chips and chicken nuggets stomped into my carpets. And even if mine were bearable, there was no guarantee their friends would be. Children move in packs. There'd be no way to avoid the mess, the chaos, the neediness, the responsibility.

Another reason why I didn't want kids, and the one I least liked to admit to, was fear. I was absolutely terrified that I'd be a bad mother – and I had good reason to think I might be.

I was seven weeks old the first time I had my heart broken. It was a Tuesday afternoon in September. It happened on an in-breath, a whisper. Silent, but significant, under a cloud-heavy sky in a green pocket of London's buzzing SE22.

While dust trucks cleared away the evidence of a long, lazy, end-of-summer weekend in the capital, black girls in beaded braids and too-short school skirts skipped home, sucking gobstoppers and avoiding the cracks in the pavement in honour of their grandmothers' superstitions. Despite the clouds, behind the door of the three-storey Victorian terrace at No. 160 Peckham Rye Road it was still warm enough for the sash windows to have been thrust upward, inviting in fat bluebottles and the hum of rush-hour traffic.

Inside, a baby girl not yet even aware she was a separate creature to her mother, lay wrapped in a yellow blanket. She closed her tiny fist around the finger of the slight, shaking young woman she had belonged to for every second of her *always* for the last time. She could not know as she searched the anguished, crumpled face to find her own that the scent she inhaled softly at night, the breast on which she suckled and sought comfort and which she believed to be her home, her heart and heartbeat would soon leave her as if she had never even existed.

Despite the gravity of the moment, the foreverness of it all, there was nothing that happened to signify this as the end, the *before* to what would come *after*. There was nothing immediately tangible or notable that marked the exact point of severance. Not an almighty thunderclap, a tremor underfoot, the sounding of an alarm or the ringing of a bell, the death knell. Nobody jotted down the time of death on that brief chapter of my young life. There was nothing, except perhaps the shuddering shoulders and swallowed guilt of a young woman who had chosen against nature, who had betrayed the bond between mother and child and, in an instant, had torn from my infant chest a piece of me that I would spend the rest of my life trying to reclaim and slot back into place. There was nothing. Nothing except the sound of footsteps leaving.

It has always seemed strange to me that I was born only 10 years after the sixties ended. It seems impossible that I arrived just 10 galactic rotations around the sun between Mary Quant's thigh-skimming minis and Catherine Bach's hazardous Daisy Dukes. It makes me feel older than I ought to. Ten years is nothing. One day you're doing the Mashed Potato and cutting a rug to Sonny and Cher and then, before you know it, you're asking the hairdresser for a Flock of Seagulls haircut and wearing out your mother's carpet practising your Electric Slide. Ten years is actually a nanosecond. It's quick-quick, blink-blink, gone in a flash.

I'm an eighties baby, born just over halfway through the first year of the decade. A DJ who the cool kids rave about released a song about being born in the eighties, about it being "acceptable". It's true that a lot of things that went down during the eighties *were* deemed acceptable at the time. Things like shoulder pads, the shooting of JR, and Milli Vanilli passing themselves off as talented vocalists and, for a while there, fooling us all. Less acceptable were things like the Aids pandemic, the Chernobyl disaster and South Africa's apartheid regime.

I was born during one the most violent periods South Africa had seen under the *oranje-blanje-blou*, the result of a most unlikely, and illegal, coupling. Probably around the same time the pre-Christmas preparations were getting underway and boughs of plastic holly were being dragged out of hard-to-reach cupboards for their annual turn in doorways and on banister rails, I was being conceived in a bunk in the staff quarters of a popular Johannesburg hotel.

My biological mother and father both worked there. She was a housekeeper, he the head chef. Their forbidden affair had begun a couple of years before I was born, starting off as a friendship of sorts. Unlikely as it seems for a white woman and a black man in South Africa, they became jogging companions and then later, in stolen moments in his modest staff accommodation and at her marital home in the suburbs, lovers.

In a real fuck-you to the hateful dogma of Hendrik Verwoerd and his motley crew of white supremacist brethren, my biological mother did the unthinkable. Against a backdrop of segregation and struggle songs, and while Vlakplaas units opened fire on opponents of PW Botha's government, the young white woman from a working-class family in the North of England and the young black man from Limpopo made the beast with two backs. Their forbidden tryst and my arrival into the world as Karoline coincided with the grand unveiling of the Rubik's Cube and Mark Chapman taking out John Lennon with four shots to the back from a .38 revolver, setting in motion a series of events that would rival the storylines of some of the eighties' best-loved soap operas.

My biological mother's husband, who delighted in the rounding out of her belly, had no idea at the time of saying "I do" that the heartbeat inside his young bride's womb wasn't, in fact, the product of his rather useless, white, cuckolded loins.

Only when I was a few weeks old and my biological father's features threatened to expose her indiscretion did my mother confess to her husband my true paternity, and together they came up with a solution that would allow them to unburden themselves of the manifestation of the sex and shame and secrets that threatened to jeopardise the future they had planned for themselves.

And so, on that Tuesday afternoon, my biological mother left me in the arms of a social worker and returned to South Africa. "She died," was the answer she gave when people asked about Baby Karoline and noticed the red rings around her eyes, her milk-heavy breasts and the empty bassinet – and *somewhere* that was true. On the day she left, my *new* parents drove up from the county of Surrey, the bastion of middle-class whiteness, to absorb me into the family they'd begun to assemble when infertility dashed their hopes of having their own children.

I often thought, before becoming a mother myself, whether having a child of my own – watching my own belly expanding and feeling the weight of new life pressing on my pelvis – would change how I felt about the decision my biological mother made back then. Would I feel any sympathy for her, some newfound understanding of the choices she made? I didn't. If anything, I was even more unable to understand how she was able to forsake her firstborn.

For a few hours after she left me that day in September 1980, I didn't belong to anyone. Until the strangers she had picked from a list to raise me, and whom she would never meet, arrived to collect me, I wasn't part of *any* family. Didn't belong anywhere or to any*one*.

Years later, I asked my adopted mum, Angela, how, as a baby, I had adjusted in the days and months after my biological mother abandoned me. "Fine," she said. Fine? Fine. Nothing noteworthy, nothing to see here, doing just *fine*. But deep down *I knew*, without question, that those empty hours and her failure to return left a blueprint on my infant psyche. I knew there was simply no way that being ripped from my mother's breast and thrust into the arms of strangers had had no impact on me whatsoever. I knew, for the same reason you're not supposed to take newborn kittens and puppies from *their* mothers, that the sudden disruption of the bond between us created a wound in me that for many years would lay fresh and pink but unseen, hidden under the veneer of my overwhelming need to appear "okay", agreeable and, of course, like so many adoptees, grateful.

At the root of it all was the fear that if I *wasn't* grateful and agreeable, then maybe my adopted parents would leave me too.

For years, I was complicit in a lie that insisted that adoption was a win-win, rainbows-and-unicorns, happily-ever-after fairy tale.

Eventually, like all wounds that are neglected and left to fester, mine became infected and the infection began to spread through the layers of epidermis until it reached the point where its stench could no longer be disguised.

Almost 29 years to the day after my biological mother left me in that house in London, I found myself wandering the City's streets. It was an early autumn evening about 18 months after I had left Enver in Cape Town. Because of his relapse, I had decided not to return to South Africa and settled back into life in the UK. I was a little over 24 months sober and had begun to rebuild my life post-rehab, post-Enver.

I was on my way to attend a lecture being held at Kensington Central Library in South West London, hosted by a psychotherapist and addictions counsellor by the name of Paul Sunderland. The lecture was titled, "Adoption and Addiction: Understanding the Impact of an Early Psychological Wound". I had no idea when I walked through the imposing wooden doors of the old red-brick building that what I was about to hear would have a profound impact on me.

"Where do we get the idea," began Sunderland, "that grief cannot be felt by babies, and trauma not experienced before one has the words to speak? It's not true."

I felt like a hand had just pulled me out from under water in which I hadn't known I was drowning.

"The separation between mother and baby unequivocally creates a wound so deep that it feels life-threatening and catastrophic to the infant," he said.

"Adoption," he went on, addressing the audience from the stage, "is a cover-up. We need to start calling it by what it is, and what it is is relinquishment, and that relinquishment is a trauma that will be felt by the adoptee for the rest of their life."

In less than five minutes Sunderland managed to give voice and credence to the, thus far, unacknowledged, but painfully evident, impact my biological mother's abandonment had had on me. For the first time in my life, here was someone speaking about it, about *adoption*, in a way that directly mirrored my own feelings and lived experiences. Saying the very things I had never been given the language for; the things that had been ignored and dismissed, the things that had been denied the space they deserved and desperately needed.

"Now, this trauma may not be remembered, but it is recalled. It has to find a way out," he explained.

I sat enthralled as Sunderland explained how adopted people were overly represented in rehabs, psychiatric facilities, jails. I was horrified when he revealed that we were considerably more likely to try to kill ourselves than those raised in their families of origin. Between me and my adopted brother, Adam, who'd taken his own life nearly 10 years before, we'd managed to tick every one of those boxes. Everything Sunderland said struck a chord with me.

"Adopted people present with a real hunger for attachment and, at the same time, a contradictory fear of rejection," explained Sunderland. "They can be neither in, nor not in, a relationship and feel regulated."

It was an aha moment.

"They are coming along to rehab with what we now call love addiction, at the end of a relationship, desperate for me to pull a rabbit out of a hat and tell them how to get back into the relationship." He was describing me to a T. *That's me, that's what I do!* I nearly leapt out of my seat. Looking around the room, I noticed several heads nodding furiously in agreement. I couldn't believe it – I wasn't the only one.

From the day I landed my first "serious" boyfriend at the age of 16, and with every single relationship, dalliance, fuck buddy and entanglement I entered into thereafter, I went in with the idea that the guy in my crosshairs *had* to be The One. Believing it was up to me to make it happen, I tried to make sure of it by being the most agreeable, desirable, reliable, malleable, fuckable girl of their dreams. Whatever it took to make them love me and, more importantly, to make sure they didn't leave me.

Nothing else mattered. It didn't *matter* how wildly inappropriate they were, how much older they were, how insolvent they were, how abusive, how emotionally unavailable, how dull, how untrustworthy, how already taken. My relationship history read like a who's who of the mean, the mad, the mercurial and the manipulative, but I was willing to put up with anything as long as they stuck around. Listening to Paul Sunderland, I realised that my poor heart had never stood a chance.

When the lecture was over, I quickly made my way outside, embarrassed that someone might see the tears of grief and rage I'd been unable to supress. I was shellshocked and felt completely let down by my adoptive parents and the flock of therapists, psychiatrists and psychologists who over the years had never connected the dots. How could they *all* have missed what was so glaringly obvious? My whole life I'd thought I was the problem. Believed I was defunct and damaged, and that I'd been born that way. And now here it was, an explanation. Something out of my control had happened to me at the most vulnerable moment of my life that had felt *life-threatening*. I wasn't an inherently bad or broken person. I was *traumatised*.

Once outside, I found a bench under a large orange horse chestnut tree within the grounds of the library. The sky had changed into its uniform for the night shift and the moon glared at me moodily through the clouds. I lit a cigarette and inhaled deeply. My chest felt thick and heavy, like when you're a kid and you stick your head out of the car window as it's flying down the highway. Too much air.

I'd spent my whole life feeling unworthy of love, craving love, terrified of *losing* love and selling myself down the river in order to *be* loved. I'd lived for years with the constant, terrifying anxiety that one wrong move could leave me abandoned again. But now it made perfect sense. If your own *mother* can leave you …

Some years later, when I met Dr Dolly, she asked me, during my primary assessment with her, whether I'd ever been diagnosed by a psychiatrist. I told her about Dr Sevcik and the bipolar diagnosis a few years before.

"It's possible," she said nodding contemplatively, "but given your history I think it's far more likely we're dealing with borderline personality disorder. They present very similarly, but the key difference is that borderline is more rooted in the psychological than the biological."

I'd gone home and read everything I could find on borderline personality disorder. There I was, in black and white: "fear of abandonment, identity disorders, defects in early mothering or chaotic parenting, self-harm, unstable relationships, suicidal ideation". I was a textbook case.

Sometimes I wonder what would happen if I were ever to return to 160 Peckham Rye Road. What would happen if I pushed open the door and walked into my past? If I held a séance on the floor of the room where the worst thing that ever happened to me happened? Would I be able to summon a ghostly memory of the moment my newborn heart broke? Would I be able to comfort the baby swaddled in the yellow blanket whose world had just disappeared in slingbacks and stonewashed denim down the steps of the Victorian tenement? And in doing so, would I be able to rewrite the chapters of my own history?

13

Have you seen my childhood?

"But *why* did you want to kill yourself, Sara-Jayne?"

Did? Past tense? Okay then.

I am 13 and at the local hospital, transported here by a wailing ambulance several hours ago, having swallowed (for what will not be the last time) a generous handful of small white pills. Each one popped, easily, through the perforated foil of two full packets I'd found in the repurposed ice-cream container our family has used as a medicine box for years and which lives in the corner cupboard above the kettle. Next to the Earl Grey.

I'd called the ambulance myself. After my initial confidence that two boxes of generic paracetamol would take me out, I soon reasoned that, in actual fact, all that was likely to happen was a crippling stomachache and some ugly vomiting. Realistically, no greater threat would be made to my young life (despite the constant warnings of my Victorian grandmother) than if I had stood outside in the biting cold with freshly washed hair in my stocking feet.

What struck me, as I stood craned over the sink on slippered tiptoes, glugging down pill after pill and listening through the kitchen door to the *Antiques Roadshow* theme tune luring my mother to her happy place, was how normal it felt doing what I was doing. Like this was a perfectly logical, proportionate response to feeling unutterably miserable. *Just kill yourself.* A default setting. In that moment and in others that would follow, it never once occurred to me that doing away with myself was something I *couldn't* do, an out I didn't have. I was genuinely surprised when, years later, I learned that not everyone feels this way.

After I downed the last pill, I sat at the piano for a few minutes staring at the sheet music for *Für Elise. Duh-duh duh-duh duh-duh duh-na-na*. When the minims began morphing into crochets and then the crochets into demi- and semiquavers, I calmly went and told my mother what I had done. I remember that she looked perplexed, not terrified or panic-stricken, but rather frustrated actually. As if my desire to do away with myself was both bewildering and inconvenient. Like the time I decided halfway through the school term that I no longer wanted to continue with cello lessons.

"Well, it's going to be very difficult to get a refund, Sara-Jayne."
exasperated sigh

I'm sitting, swinging my feet, on an orange plastic NHS chair in the appallingly decorated and patronisingly named "Little Grown-Ups" room in the children's ward. Mickey Mouse, inexplicably dressed in a tuxedo and top hat, is doing cartwheels across one wall, while a blonde, tiara-wearing princess strokes the face of a bewildered-looking unicorn on the other. It's too much.

I turn away from Mickey and the unicorn whisperer to the doctor who, even at my tender age, seems alarmingly young. Like Doogie Howser. I loved that show. The doctor leans in towards me, resting his forearms on his knees in a move I guess he has been taught is "non-threatening". As he moves, his tie flops forward and I'm able to make out the image of Bart Simpson on a skateboard under a speech bubble that reads, "Cowabunga, dudes!" I grip the underside of the chair, thankfully free of discarded chewing gum, and do my best not to look Doogie (or Bart) directly in the eye.

I'm terrified of these types of grown-ups. Ones who want to "get down to my level" or introduce themselves as "just a big kid myself really", like somehow that's a good thing. Adults should stick to being adults. I am terrified of childlike behaviour in grown-ups. I already have enough of that at home.

Things at home are difficult. We have "family problems". That's what you're supposed to say at school when the teacher asks why you haven't done your homework again and you don't want to get into it in front of your 30-strong, eager-eared bunch of classmates. If you say "family problems" they leave it at that and instead ask to speak to you "privately" after class or at home time.

What I understand, from my 13-year-old perspective, is that *our* family problems started about three years ago, about 18 years into my parents' marriage. Youth had, until recently, offered me the protection of being self-absorbed enough not to have noticed the cracks that had almost certainly been appearing in their relationship long before that, but about three years ago is when I first became aware of it becoming harder to breathe at home. Like the air was being sucked out of the house.

Like most children, I'm unable to see my mum and dad outside of being my parents, and the thought that they existed, either as a couple or as individuals, prior to the arrival of Adam and me is unimaginable.

It's *because* I can only see them as my parents that I'm unable to appreciate how unsurprising their imminent divorce is. Had I perhaps known them both in the early seventies, when they met, I might well have urged them to reconsider walking down the aisle.

My parents are very different people from very different backgrounds. Mum comes from a wealthy upper-middle-class family from Surrey. As a child, she'd been driven to her private school in a private car by her grandfather's private chauffeur. Dad is a coalminer's son from the North of England who moved

117

down south as soon as he turned 18 to escape the inevitability of following his father underground.

When they married, they wanted to have four children but struggled for years to conceive. Eventually when they did, my mother lost the baby a few weeks into the pregnancy. Finally, they decided that the only option left was to adopt, and that's how they ended up with Adam and me.

For a long time, we've put on a convincing performance of *Happy Families*. Dad, an engineer, earns a good wage, and Mum, who only returned to work when Adam and I were older, spends her days fixing messed-up families through her job as a child-protection social worker.

I've come as close to perfecting the role of "the good daughter" as I can and have done my best to prove my worth by doing well in school and being agreeable. I've really tried to squeeze my little square black peg into the whitewashed round hole that circumstance has dictated is my lot, but it's excruciatingly obvious – to me, at least – that I just don't fit.

Adam, not terribly academic, has showed that his prowess is on the sports field (his bedroom is filled with trophies from his sports day victories), but to my mum's distress and my dad's fury, he's considered one of the "naughty boys" at school and is no stranger to detention.

None of us ever speaks of our personal tragedies and traumas. Adam and I because we don't have the language for them, and Mum and Dad because they just aren't *those* kinds of people.

For the most part, we've stuck to the script, but then the year before last, after a tense few months that saw my parents doing lots of talking through gritted teeth, some painfully silent suppers and Dad spending a night on our next-door neighbour's sofa, he announced, on Christmas Day, that he and Mum were splitting up. Since then, things have rapidly gone downhill.

Dad packed his bags and moved out and he's now living

with Sarah, the woman who used to do our ironing and polish Granny's silver. It's been months since I last saw him. I spend a lot of time wondering what more I could have done to stop him from leaving. I also spend a lot of time pondering whether it's normal practice that, when people split up, they divorce their kids as well.

Almost as bad as Dad not being around any more is the fact that we've had to move house. The rambling farm where I spent my formative years and into whose fields I could escape when the house became a pressure cooker had to be sold ("to pay your mother's solicitor", said Dad) and home is now a little cottage in a neighbouring village. Most of the time, it's just Mum and me who live there, but it's too small. No one seemed to take account of all the extra room we'd need for our unspoken suffering.

Mum cries a lot. When she cries, I feel helpless. And useless. The more she cries, the more helpless and useless (and scared) I feel. I also know I'm not making things any easier. Recently, I've been caught bunking school and Mum has been called in to speak to the Head of Year. They want to know why I'm playing truant and I don't have an answer. They're the adults – aren't they supposed to know?

What I'm doing doesn't *feel* like playing truant or bunking. Bunking is what Adam and his friends do when they want to smoke weed, drink cheap cider and pass around each other's porn magazines in the park when they should be in double science. I'm not doing that. I'm just not going to school. There's no joy in not going. No fun. Mostly, what I do when I sneak back home and let myself in with the spare key after Mum goes to work, is climb back into bed and pull the duvet over my head. I do that, and I eat. In addition to the books I've been consuming for years, I've recently discovered that food can provide a similar type of comfort and escape.

I feel terrible that I'm making life difficult for Mum, on top of everything else that's going on. She needs me to be the good girl I've always been. I can tell she doesn't understand where her usually easy and amenable child has gone, but I don't either. I can't quite work out if she's more disappointed for me or for her. I think she's angry with me. She hasn't yet said it outright, but I know she wishes I'd just pull myself together.

The other day I overheard her on the phone.

"She's getting fat. Just sits around eating all the time."

And it's true, I am, and I do. Sometimes, after I've walked back home from the bus stop, having watched dozens of my uniform-clad classmates heading to school, I go home and I just eat. Full of shame at once again not having been able to summon the courage to get on the bus and go to school like a normal kid, I eat. I don't even bother to change out of my uniform. I just loosen the tie from around my throat, sit on the floor of the kitchen and inhale food in the futile hope that it'll fill the hole in my soul. Sometimes I don't even wait for the food to thaw or heat. I just eat and eat and eat.

The worst part is that I don't know *why* I can't go to school. Every morning I slip on my white shirt, my tie in house colours, climb into my non-regulation, above-the-knee blue skirt and slide my arms into my navy blazer boasting the school shield and the motto *"Fortiter Fideliter"*. But as I stand staring at my reflection, I don't *feel* strong and faithful. I feel terror and shame. Because I know that, despite going through the motions of laying out my uniform and packing my schoolbag the night before, I won't go. I *can't* go. The conclusion I come to is that there's obviously something wrong with me. I don't know why I'm not normal, like my friends. I don't know why I feel everything so acutely all the time. As usual, I'm being oversensitive. Mum's right – I ought to pull myself together.

Soon I will be expelled from school for non-attendance. When it happens, it will become almost impossible to ignore the disappointment reverberating off my mother's shoulders. I will watch as the hope drains from her grey, falling face that she'll ever be able to answer anything other than "she's a troubled lass" when her friends pityingly ask how I am. It's a look, one of helplessness and disappointment, that I've seen before; it's the same look she wore when Adam had begun to "go off the rails".

Like Dad, Adam also lives somewhere else now. Three years older and one pair of Nike Air Max trainers cooler than me, he has spent the last few years proving that the apple really doesn't fall far from the tree. He's apparently inherited *his* biological mother's desire to escape into the bottle and, at almost 16, he is already a fully fledged, often violent alcoholic.

He's been in and out of foster care for two years because Mum can't cope with him. I know this because she tells me she can't cope. She also tells me that because it's just the two of us, we need to "look after each other". When she says this, I get the same feeling as when I'm standing in front of the school bus in the morning. Like my heart is pumping in my stomach and not my chest. Like I might faint. I want to scream, "You're the parent – *you* need to look after *me*!"

Whenever Adam *does* come home, I have to lock my bedroom door because otherwise he steals my things. Money, jewellery, clothes, CDs. Anything he can pawn to get money, which he then spends on alcohol. When he leaves again, I have to do an inventory of my stuff. Sometimes I can't even work out what he's taken – I can just *sense* that something's missing. The absolute violation of him stealing from me breaks my heart. Even if it's for alcohol, I'd sooner give him the money willingly. When he's drunk, the house gets even smaller. Sometimes we have to call the police.

There have been other violations, other things he's taken from me in the last two years that can't be sold, but I don't tell Mum about that stuff. He's my brother and I love him, but I don't like some of the things he does.

It starts as normal sibling antics. Horseplay between brother and sister. But then one day the playful jostling, the grabbing, the hitting and poking becomes something else. It's a Sunday evening. My mother is downstairs, sitting on the reupholstered chaise longue, eating overfilled egg mayonnaise sandwiches while watching *Poirot*. We are upstairs. I'm 10, he's 12 going on 13. I have been allowed in his bedroom to watch the small, crackly, black-and-white TV he bought with his birthday money. There are fresh sheets on the bed and the carpet is newly vacuumed, but the room still smells like the lost-property box at school. Musty, pubescent. A number of different funks vying for dominance among the discarded soccer boots and model aeroplanes. Because it's his room, I have to do what he says. Those are the rules. I must sit where he tells me to sit; I'm not allowed to touch anything, look at anything, without his permission.

"Move up," he says.

We are sitting on his bed, him leaning against the headboard, my back against the wall, legs hanging off the side of the bed. I shuffle an inch to the right.

"More," he says and kicks the small of my back with his foot. I slap his foot away. He kicks again. I throw One-Eyed Ted at him.

He grins and punches me in the arm.

"I'll tell Mum," I say, grinning back.

He pinches me, I pinch him back.

"I'm gonna tell," I warn.

He pinches again, this time on my budding chest. It hurts.

"Boobies, boobies!" he sings.

"Mum!" I shout. "Adam's hitti—", but before I can finish he's pulled both pillows out from behind him and launched one at me.

"Pillow fight!" he challenges.

I manage to get in a few weak blows before he overpowers me. He straddles my waist and turns my head into the duvet. I inhale the fabric conditioner as I feel the weight of him on top of me. Cherry blossom. Something in his shorts is hard and hurting me.

I want to call Mum again, but she'll be cross if I interrupt her programme.

He moves faster and harder on top of me until Mum calls up the stairs and tells me it's bath time.

Later, as I'm getting undressed, I wonder how I managed to get mayonnaise, white and creamy, on the front of my shorts.

A few weeks after the first time, Dad pulls up outside the house to fetch me. It is his weekend. He sounds the horn and I grab my school bag – now repurposed into an overnight-at-Dad's bag – and scuttle out the front door. I half-run, half-walk down the path and scoot into the front seat of his mustard-yellow Austin Maxi, shoving the bag down into the footwell between my feet. It's summer and my legs are sticking to the tan leather seats. I slide my hands under my thighs and morph into the version of myself that I know Dad finds most pleasing.

An hour or so later, we arrive at his new place, and as I'm about to climb out of the car, I notice a box full of books on the back seat.

"They're for you," says Dad, "from Sarah."

Sarah is often passing things on for him to give to me. Things her own two teenage daughters no longer want or have outgrown. Last month it was a pair of brown pixie boots, today it's books.

Dad pulls his seatbelt forward and reaches around into the

back. He takes a book from the top of the box. It's called *Understanding the Facts of Life*. It has several cartoon drawings on the cover. One is of a heavily pregnant woman, another of a young couple holding hands. A cartoon bird and a cartoon bee are perched on the letters of the title. Dad tosses the book into my lap and says abruptly, "I'll talk to you about most things, but not about sex!" He climbs out of the car and walks towards the house. I don't move. I stay sitting in the car, the book on my knees. What he doesn't realise is that I already know about sex.

I forgave my brother, instantly, for the things he did, *all* of them, because I know how it feels to be drawn to do something you think will make you feel better, but once you've done it, actually makes you feel worse. Even if no one else was able to say it, we were living difficult lives, he and I. I would also learn to forgive him when, years later, the living became too difficult and he a put a dog chain around his neck and hanged himself from a bridge.

At the hospital, they have, mercifully, allowed me to get dressed, back into my own clothes, the ones I was wearing when I arrived last night with a stomach full of chalky white tablets and a backpack full of shame and regret. Hospital gowns are horror shows and akin to wearing a large, ill-fitting napkin. I am years away (in either direction) from not giving a shit about complete strangers being able to see my bare ass.

"Why did you want to kill yourself?"

It's a fair question. Why *did* I want to kill myself? Did. Do. Tom-ay-to. Tom-ah-to.

I stare at Dr Doogie (the *actual* Doogie had a far less ridiculous haircut).

"Okay," he says, patting both palms on his Levi's. "Okay, let's do this. Can you tell me three things that make you happy?"

I can't, so I say nothing.

"Anything you like," he tries again with a reassuring smile. Thankfully, he holds back from telling me "there are no right answers here", else I'd be likely to run head-first into Mickey and his monkey suit on the opposite wall.

"Okay, how about we start with just *two* things?"

How the fuck was Doogie Howser legally allowed to practise medicine when he was only 16 years old?

"Okay, I'll start. The three things that make *me* happy are chess, walks in the park and flying my remote-control aeroplane."

Jesus Christ.

"Your turn."

I mean, regardless of whether he'd had the intellectual capacity to pass the medical exams, what kind of cowboy-run hospital would think it's a good idea to actually employ a fucking teenager to treat members of the public?

"Okay, o*ne* thing. *One* thing that makes you happy?"

Like, what if he'd killed someone, because he was tired from staying up all night playing Super Mario World on his Game Boy or jerking his barely pubescent cock to some big-titted 19-year-old bombshell in Playboy?

"You know, Sara-Jayne, we *really* do want to help you."

I mean, 16-year-old boys should be allowed the freedom of a late-night wank without the pressure of knowing they may accidentally kill someone the next day if they don't get their full eight hours a night.

"Okay, we'll leave it here for now. We can talk some more when your mum gets here later." There's a resigned sigh.

Kids should be allowed to be kids, I think as Doogie and Bart exit stage left.

14

A pregnant pause

There is blood everywhere. Luminous, deep maroon, wet. In some places, where it has been given time and air to breathe, it's rust-coloured and congealing. Some of it has begun to pool in the depression my legs have made in the blankets. I am sitting, legs crossed, as if to meditate. For me, this is meditation. The release and flow, release and flow. The slackening of the bow, the silent, bloody exhale, the loosening of the taut skin across the relentless, beating drum with its persistent duh-dom duh-dom duh-dom, *to which, no matter how hard I try, I can never keep time. If I'm not careful, it will beat me until I'm dead.*

I tilt my forearm to inspect my handiwork and, as I do, a tear-sized drop drip-drips and lands perfectly on the pillow propping up my left knee. "Tears on my pillow," I whisper and watch as it seeps, its vivid stain trespassing outward on the white cotton.

I angle my arm upward, this time letting rivulets of red track their bloody way from my elbow down onto the bedclothes. It's coming nicely now. Flowing. My lifeblood. I love the feeling of it. A strange mix of warm and cold. It feels like the softest length of velvet being drawn over my skin. Liquid pain.

It's been years since the last time. But it was always still there. Dormant. My last card to be played when the table was about to see and trounce my hand. Years of highs and lows, triumphs and tragedies, heartbreaking loves and losses, weight gains and thigh gaps, deaths and rebirths, moments of serenity and eternities of chaos. I have flown over oceans and back again, cried across continents and replanted roots in the land of my birth. I have climbed stairs in the steeples of churches whose religions I despise, and I have felt the ringing of gongs through the souls of my feet. I have isolated and silenced myself for days in a bid for repose and screamed at the edge of the sea until my lungs caught fire and still not enough time has passed to allow me to forget. I can never forget, because I literally have the scars to prove it.

After a couple of minutes, the addict needs another hit. The first is wearing off. I lie back and take a deep breath. On the exhale, I take the blade against my thumb and press the flat of it along my forefinger. I stretch out my arm and where history has left room on the wounded canvas, in between the scars of yesterdays and once-upon-a-times, I place the cold metal against my skin, press down hard and pull.

I do it again, but this time I press harder. I do it another three, four, five, six times. Each time, as blade meets flesh, my chest releases and there is a rush of something warm, electric, liquid and light. It pours itself over my shoulders, down through my limbs, and pools, simmering, in my hands and feet. It washes up over the back of my neck and, as it does, my head slumps back, my arm drops against my side and my eyelids begin to droop. This is what I've been waiting for. This is what I needed to remind me. To remind me what it feels like to feel. What it feels like to be alive.

I wake with a start, heart *ta-ta-ta-ta-ta*, hammering against my chest, a furious metronome. I heave myself to sitting, floundering in the dark in the space next to the bed, desperate for light but also terrified of what it will reveal. I'm expecting to see a shock of red, my nightclothes stained crimson with my own defeat.

I locate the chord of the bedside lamp and monkey my fingers up to its switch. *Click*. A fluorescent halo of light fills the space around the bed. Without waiting for my eyes to adjust, I shift awkwardly, first patting the sheet underneath me, then balancing on my right arm so I can thrust my left closer to the light. Nothing. I run my fingertips along my skin. Just to make sure. Nothing. Only the wounds of the past. Nothing that speaks of my most recent hurts. I'm as relieved as I can be.

I'm getting used to being woken up like this. "Using dreams", we call them in recovery. I've had them ever since I got clean. They used to happen a lot in the early days, and it would terrify me how real they seemed. Sometimes they were so vivid that I'd wake up with the taste of alcohol on my tongue or the smell of blood in my nostrils. But then the days had turned into months had turned into years and they just didn't happen as often. Once a year would be a lot. I've been in The Clinic for almost a week now and I've had them every single night. I'm relieved when I wake up, but then I remember where I am, and why, and wish that it could be a very different nightmare I've woken up from.

I swing my legs out from under the duvet and place my feet flat on the cold floor. In the dim light I can see the shape of my roommate contentedly cocooned in her own duvet on the other side of the room. She'll enjoy another four or five hours like that at least, thanks to the combo of Valium and Stilnox she knocks back every night at the nurse's station. I envy her.

On her bedside table is a small, ornate picture frame. In the light of day, it holds a photograph of her, her husband and her young daughter, all grinning happily at the camera in Technicolor, but right now all I'm able to make out are three shadowy figures peering ominously at me from across the room.

It's been seven days since Enver confessed his sins and revealed that our whole life was a lie. The only thing that's real is that I'm carrying his baby and I'm completely alone. There are times when I think the pain might actually kill me. Everything hurts. The soles of my feet, the whites of my eyes, the quick of my nails. It hurts to breathe, so I hold my breath, but that hurts too. I can feel it sucking the air out of my lungs.

Every time I think I'm still numb from shock, the pain hits hard and heavy. It's the sheer weight of it, like being trapped under an enormous boulder, its bulk bearing down so that I'm unable to edge myself out, the air slowly being pressed out of me. I fear it will suffocate me in my sleep, like an intruder clamping a hand over my mouth and nose. Sometimes, when it seems there is no space left inside me in which to hold it, I'm struck by a sense of emptiness so profound that it's like I've been gutted, my insides scraped out of me with a buck knife. Gralloched like a deer.

It's not just the pain; it's also the fear. I am more scared than I have ever been in my entire life. I *know* I *cannot* do this. I cannot, on my own, birth and raise a child. I'm not built that way. I don't have the mettle for it. Whatever it is that some people have inside them to do this alone is missing in me. I know this for a fact.

All the years I ruled out becoming a mother, my *biggest* fear was that I'd inherited something from my birth mother that meant I might *also* be capable of abandoning my children. Even though the idea of it was completely contrary to who I was as a person, who was to say that the *thing*, whatever it was, that gave her the ability to walk away from me didn't live in the very marrow of my bones or the structure of my DNA?

"It's all about your own abandonment – *you* need to parent your inner child," a friend who was studying psychology suggested once, and she was probably on to something. For a long time, my inner child had been running the show and the result was unremitting chaos. I'd spent my adult life desperate for security and attachment, but at the same time running from responsibility and intimacy. Once, when I told a friend I was thinking of getting a dog, she'd shrieked incredulously, "A dog! You can't even look after yourself!" I was absolutely crushed. But maybe she was right?

The responsibility of parenthood terrified me. As a child, I often felt it was *my* responsibility to look after my mum. Sometimes I'd sit helpless as she sobbed or fretted about my brother's drinking and delinquency, and I'd feel like we had swapped roles. Years later I made the connection between that time of my life and my aversion to vulnerability and neediness in others. When Adam *was* at home, it felt as if I was co-parenting him with her. I wondered later whether my tendency to choose partners much older than me was a way of (as it turns out, unsuccessfully) trying to make sure no one was expecting me to be Mummy. I didn't have the tools nor the inclination to fix someone else's emotional *owies*. And so, for a long, long time, motherhood just wasn't a risk I was prepared to take.

But then, as I got older, things began to change. As much as I enjoyed my independence, the freedom of being able to do as I pleased, to revel in being the centre of my own universe, the thought that I might *never* have a family of my own, made me uneasy. Even some of my most defiantly non-mumsy friends were having kids and when I looked at them, I was envious, I wanted what they had. I wanted a *family*.

I started to daydream about a house filled with love and laughter and Lego. Lazy Sunday lie-ins in a huge bed filled with kids and dogs and one-armed action figures. I wanted the chance to create the type of family mine could have been had it not been torn asunder by dysfunction and divorce.

When Enver and I spoke about having children, slowly the fear that I might have inherited the rejection gene from my birth mother began to dissipate. I wouldn't be doing it alone, I reasoned. I'd have a partner, a teammate, someone to back me up, to celebrate the triumphs and console me in the tribulations. Someone to share the joy but also the intensity and terror of parenthood.

It was never about wanting just to have a *baby*, I wanted a *family*. But that's all over now, the possibility gone up in smoke, and I feel as ill equipped for what's to come as I did as a child wiping away my mother's tears.

It's been six days and I've heard nothing from Enver since the day I arrived at The Clinic. He sent a message saying he wanted to come and visit.

SJ: Visiting hours are between 6 and 8, but you need to be clean if you come here.

Enver: I'll come. I just want you to settle in for a bit.

SJ: I don't need to "settle in", Enver. More likely you're not clean. Don't come if you're not. Don't bring your chaos here.

Enver: I'll visit on Friday.

That was Monday. If he was going to detox, he would need at least five days with the junk out of his system to produce a clean drug test.

SJ: Suit yourself, but you need to be clean. I'm dead serious, Enver.

I hoped I sounded "dead serious". The right amount of vitriol. But Enver wasn't the only one I was trying to convince.

Enver: I'm coming on Friday.

SJ: Whatever, Enver, just don't come here with your nonsense.

Friday has come and gone, with no sign of Enver.

After two weeks, my time at The Clinic is up. Two weeks is how long I'd given myself when I checked in. My medical aid will pay for three, but I decide it would be provident to save a few days, just in case. For insurance. I can't imagine not having The Clinic as a safety net, although I don't know what the rules are about bringing a baby into a psychiatric facility. Fucking hell, is that who I'm going to be now? A single, mentally unstable mother, checking in and out of madhouses with a baby on her breast?

I don't want to go, is what I think as I sign my way through the discharge forms and shuffle heavily out of High Care, wheeling my baggage behind me. I don't want to go because, as soon as I step outside, I'll have to face everything in the stark and assaulting brightness of day.

Once I'm home, I do my best to slip back into real life but, as I'd feared, there is no let-up from the despair. It is with me constantly. I carry it through the day like an oversized cloak and fall into bed at night, exhausted, where it covers me like a weighted blanket.

I've only confided in a few people about what's going on and while everyone's being as supportive as they know how, nothing anyone says provides me with any comfort. I know they mean well, but all I want is for someone to say something that will make the pain go away. Instead, they say things like, "Just focus on the baby" and "You don't need him, loads of women do this on their own" or, worst of all, "You have to hold it together for *her* sake", which makes me feel as if *I* don't matter at all and that I'm just the seedbed for the life I'm growing inside me. The fact is, I *can't* focus on the baby and I'm *not* holding it together.

No one would ever hold a man to the same grit-your-teeth-and-bear-it standards, and I realise for the first time that there's no such thing as the *magic mother gene*. I've fallen victim to the patriarchal lie that suggests there's something in the make-up of people born with a womb and a vagina that gives us the ability to gird our loins and *byt vas* through any storm. Maternal instinct is *not* the same thing as enforced maternal fortitude.

Others try a different approach – "He'll come round once he sees the baby" and "This will be what makes him finally get himself together" – but their false assurances just make me even more depressed because I know addiction doesn't work like that.

When I share how scared I am of looking after the baby on my own, people swear they'll come and help – "We'll set up a roster!", "You'll never been on your own!", "Just try keeping me away!" – but, despite their kind promises, I know no one is coming to rescue me.

I'm deeply depressed, but I've been off all my medications since we started trying for the baby. It's the first time in 12 years I haven't taken anything, but I refuse to take Dr Dolly up on her offer to prescribe me something. "I'm okay," I'd insisted in The Clinic, even though it was patently clear that I wasn't. But I'm already a bad mother, so it's unthinkable that I will also now risk harming the baby just so I can avoid feeling the pain of a situation I've failed to protect us from. My suffering is the very least punishment I deserve.

Faced with the prospect of being the sole financial provider for the baby and because I now have a bond to pay, I throw myself into work. Every day, seven days a week, until the baby arrives. It's utterly exhausting, but it also keeps my mind busy and provides windows of brief but welcome respite from the horror of what's happening.

Even though the transfer has gone through on the house, I still haven't left Sheila's because I can't stand the thought of being in my new place on my own. Most of the time, when I get back from work, I disappear straight into my bedroom with my grief and wait for sleep to come.

Eventually, I know, I'll have to move out, just like I know that in a few months' time I'll have to give birth. The house thing is marginally easier to face, and in my spare time I begin decorating and filling it up room by room, transforming it from a bland beige box into a space I think might be able to tolerate when, in a few months' time, I'm trapped within its walls, on my own, with a screaming baby.

I also know that I ought to be preparing for *her* arrival, but so far, each time I've gone to the mall with the intention of buying burp cloths and bootees and bum cream, I've ended up leaving with nothing. Twice now I've abandoned a trolley full of baby paraphernalia and fled the store in tears because the sight of an expectant couple excitedly stocking up on Pampers and a young dad gleefully cooing into a pram had knocked the wind right out of me. It had taken everything in me not to scream out loud with the sadness and unfairness of it all.

Physically though, I'm doing well. At five months, I'm starting to show, and every three weeks the bump and I make our way to see Dr Wondimu, who is pleased with how things are progressing. I have to steel myself to make the trip, because it's where I feel Enver's absence most keenly. I try to arrive at least two minutes late, to minimise the risk of encountering happy couples skipping out of Wondimu's room clutching their scans. I've heard nothing from Enver since my first day at The Clinic and even though he never asks me where Enver is (which is a relief, since I don't know), I think Wondimu can read from my stricken face that things are bad. His kindness and calming manner are comforting and reassuring, and sometimes I'm so grateful for them that it brings me to tears right there on his examination table.

One day, when I'm about 23 weeks along, I'm at work, preparing to start my show. Mercifully, I'm no longer doing the gruelling late-night slot and have been given a more agreeable weekend gig. I'm about to drive the red mic fader up to go live, when I feel something. A flicker, no, a flutter on the left side of my growing belly. Instinctively, I put my hand down to feel. Another flutter. And then another! "Hello ..." it seems to say.

For the first time, it dawns on me that while I've been in a state of paralysis for the last few weeks since Enver's disappearance, the baby knows nothing of the madness and is just getting on with the business of growing into the next fruit.

The thought brings a smile to my face, and I rub my belly again. Another flutter. I push the fader up and the red on-air light illuminates. "Hello, and welcome!" I say into the mic.

Later, after the show, I'm taking some things over to the new house when I find myself taking the turn-off to the mall. I head straight back to the shop I'd bolted from a week earlier. "One thing," I tell myself. "Just get *one* thing for the baby and then you can go." On an impossibly small, pink hanger I see a tiny, sleeveless, cream-and-fuchsia-pink one-piece with gold stripes. It's garish. It's gauche. I love it. I take it to the till and hand my card over to the cashier. "I'm having a baby," I tell her. She smiles back at me, polite but indifferent. When I get to the new house, I take the babygro out of the bag, flop down on the sofa and place it over my bump.

"Hello, baby," I say out loud.

15

LDN, DXB, CPT

I need to get out of Cape Town. Enver and I are all over this city and its proximity to my grief is suffocating. I can't go anywhere without being reminded of the time, just a few months ago, when I thought I was happy. Before my world fell apart. There's no escape from the memories of the past, the dread of the future or the unrelenting agony of the present. I need some distance to pretend what is happening is not happening.

I've decided to visit my mum in the UK and on my way back spend some time in Dubai, a city I called home once upon a time. The Cape Town winter has begun to put a chill in my bones, and I figure I can thaw out in the desert for a few days. I need to go *now*, I tell myself, before the baby gets here and I'm grounded forever.

I'm bracing myself for life as I know it being over, unable to imagine how I will ever be happy again. I'm also guilt-ridden by the fact that I am still struggling to feel any real excitement or joy for what's to come. Although, I suspect it's not that I *don't* feel *any*, but rather that the noise of everything else is so loud that it drowns it out completely. I hate myself for feeling this way. I hate Enver for making me feel this way. I hate him for robbing me of the capacity to be happy about something that should be so joyous; in fact, I hate him for robbing me of the capacity to be happy about anything at all these days.

I book my ticket to London, dubbing the trip my "last hurrah". I say it with a big, fat, fake smile on my face and work it into the daily performance of "delighted expectant mother" that I've begun to put on at work. It's a challenging role, but one for which I could quite deservedly win a Best Actress award. Because I'm now showing and unable to avoid the "Congratulations!" and "When are you due?", I've had to embark on an exhausting PR offensive of being *happy happy happy!* when, in reality, a little more of my spirit, and my heart, breaks every day.

A lot of the time I'm just going through the motions, moving through life on autopilot. Doing the things the pregnancy apps, mom-to-be websites and endless *you've-got-a-bun-in-the-oven* Instagram accounts tell me I should be doing. I've realised it's easier to rely on non-interactive sources of information than on the flesh-and-blood advice of friends or well-meaning colleagues, which is too much, too personal. When anyone IRL beams at my belly and offers me unsolicited words of wisdom on heartburn, swollen ankles and the constant fucking peeing, I want to claw their eyes out of their goddamn skulls.

Despite my intentions, the trip to London isn't as helpful at giving me a break from the stress as I'd hoped. My mum and I, who have a difficult relationship, are as usual unable to meet one another in a non-defensive space and things are fraught from the second I land. Ours is another relationship in which the unspoken traumas of the past are continually at play in the present. We're a textbook case for why adoptive families ought to be required to undergo therapy from day one. Too much pain and no safe space for it to be allowed to breathe. The result is a powder keg of hurt.

I've also been aware for a while that, as someone who was never able to have her own children, my mum might be going through her own difficult and painful experience of my pregnancy.

"Do you think she might be jealous?" an adopted friend of mine asked just before I told Mum I was expecting.

"Truthfully? I don't know," I replied. "It's possible, and honestly, totally understandable. I'd get it if she were. It's just not something I'd ever be able to ask her. We don't have that kind of relationship. It makes me sad."

And it's true – we just don't have that kind of relationship. I remember the first time my mother told me she loved me. I was 19 and it was about two months after my brother died. It's a memory so vivid in my mind that I remember exactly where and what I was doing when it happened. Nineteen years is a long time.

I arrive at Heathrow, tired, sore and emotionally in a million little pieces. I desperately want Mum to fling her arms tight around me so I can hang onto her and scream my pain into her shoulders. I want her to tell me it will all be okay; I want her to tell me I'll be an amazing mother (even if she doesn't believe it) and that she'll be right by my side every step of the way. I want her to rage at Enver and his family on my behalf and feel my pain as if it's *her* pain. But she doesn't and it hurts.

The next day I have lunch with Josie, an old recovery friend who's been "in the rooms" for close to 20 years and is a poster child for self-awareness and healing. She's always full of wise words and sage advice. I tell her how I'm feeling about my mother.

"Ah, you see, but you've done it again," she says when I'm done ranting.

"Done what?" I say, pushing away a plate of beautifully poached salmon that looked delicious on the menu but which the baby has now decided is a definite no-go.

"You've ramped your expectations up to 100, when history tells you you're only ever going to 50."

"But she's my *mum*!"

"And?" Josie sips her lemon water.

"And she's *supposed* to … She's meant to … *Why* doesn't she …?" My eyes are threatening to embarrass me in this far-too-posh-for-me French bistro.

"Because she can't," she says, simply but kindly.

"Doesn't she love me?"

"I'm sure she loves you, but she can't give what she doesn't have. What do I always say about expectations?"

"That they are the mother of all resentments," I recite back to her sadly.

"Yup. Now, are you going to eat that salmon or can I take it home for the dogs?"

Five days later, while Mum's driving me back to the airport, the tensions that have been brewing for the duration of my stay finally erupt. I've tried, clumsily, to tell her how I feel, but what ensues is the usual melee of tears, shouting, accusations and denials. We're simply not able to meet in a place of vulnerability and honesty. She pulls up at Passenger Drop-Off and, with tears flowing, chest heaving and heart breaking, I slam the car door and lug my bags and my bulk towards Departures. Josie is right. I have broken my own cardinal rule when it comes to my mother. Up in the air, I sob all the way from LHR to DXB. We won't speak again until after the baby is born.

As soon as I land in the desert, I realise that this is not the same place I once knew and called home. I barely recognise it any more and sense that it feels the same way about me. Key landmarks remain, of course, but entire suburbs and cities within a city have risen in my absence. It's unnerving, in a way, but it's also just Dubai, always morphing. Unless you know exactly where to look, it's very difficult to find the true heart of the place.

Big cities have always scared me – I think because I'm really a country girl at heart and most comfortable in wide-open spaces, listening to silence. As someone who grew up on a farm, moving at nature's pace, the urban jungle, with its frenetic energy and fast talk, is yet another place where I've always felt I have to morph into another version of myself in order to fit in. The contradiction is that big cities also excite me. Like roller coasters. When I find myself in one, I have to strap in and make sure I fall in at the right rhythm to avoid whiplash.

I'd moved to Dubai from London nearly 15 years before to "start anew". To the outside world, I framed it as a strategic career move, but in reality I desperately wanted to shake the ever-present sense of worthlessness, discontent and agitation that seemed to follow me around like bad smell.

But things didn't work out in the desert as I'd hoped. I was miserable and discontent, drinking too much and battling a rampant eating disorder (just as I had been in England). I was eventually fired from my job at Radio Dubai and life looked bleak. I took my sacking as a sign and, combined with the demise of my sexless, co-dependent relationship with a kind, sexually unappealing computer geek, I decided it was as good a time as any to take myself out of circulation for a while and flew to South Africa to go to rehab.

While there, it was suggested that my move to Dubai had been a "geographical" and that it was pretty much a rite of passage for addicts like me – the mistaken belief that we can cure our addictions with a "fresh start" in a new place. It doesn't work, because needless to say, "Wherever you go, there you are."

"It's about as useful as changing deckchairs on the *Titanic*," my rehab therapist told me in our first one-on-one session. It was a revelation. It had genuinely never occurred to me that what I was always trying to run away from was me.

After a few days of browning my bump under the unforgiving sun, floating blissfully in the warm waters of the Gulf and making amends with a city I'd once professed to hate "with every fibre of my body", I start to think that maybe I could move back to Dubai. Just me and the baby. Start afresh. I get as far as picturing myself pushing a pram through the Mall of the Emirates or the two of us playing in the sand in the shadow of the Burj Al Arab, before I remember that wherever you go, there you are, and that *houses built on sand* …

Prior to leaving for England, I had been praying for a let-up in the grief that had me bound, and then one day, just before I left, it came. But the grief was replaced with something else, something even bigger. Rage. Searing and absolute. Demanding its own time in the spotlight, the anger came in hard. Ferocious, loud and unruly.

I harboured a hatred for Enver bordering on the psychopathic. I fantasised about him coming to harm. To feel the pain I was feeling, but a million times worse. And not just Enver, his family too. I hated them with an intensity that vibrated through my whole body. Sometimes I hated them more than I did him. He's off his head on heroin, I thought, but what's their excuse?

I'd messaged Enver's mother the day I arrived at The Clinic. We'd never enjoyed a close relationship, but in all the years I'd known her I'd had no reason to suspect she didn't like me. From my room in High Care, I'd revealed to her everything Enver had confessed, expecting her to be as dumbfounded as I was, but she hadn't appeared shocked, just weary and distant.

"I'm sorry that you are going through this and just pray you stay strong for you and the baby."

After that, I didn't hear from her again. I couldn't understand it. Enver might have been an eternal disappointment to her, but I'm not Enver, the baby is not Enver. We were separate to *his* chaos. Why couldn't *we* still be a part of that big, supposedly happy family? The same one that just a few weeks previously had pushed me into shot for a "Say cheese!" family photo opportunity.

Two days before leaving The Clinic, I sent his mother *another* message.

"It would be really nice to know that you care about me and the baby. Even just to pick up the phone and ask how I'm doing in light of everything that has happened."

Nothing.

I also reached out to another of Enver's family members, but it soon became clear that I was the one with egg on her face because everyone, it seemed, had known about his using all along. That's why he didn't want to tell his mother about the baby, because she knew – they *all* knew – what was really going on. But if they knew, why did no one say anything? Did they assume I *knew*? And if they did, did they honestly think I would knowingly have a baby with someone in active heroin addiction?

The anger and injustice of it started to pulse in the centre of my forehead, right between my eyes. Unable to stop myself, I sent *another* message.

"I've known your family for 12 years. I cannot understand what I could possibly have done to YOU that would make you ignore me the way you have done over the past few months. To not even reach out to ask if me and your unborn grandchild are okay. What could I possibly have done to deserve that?"

Nothing.

Enraged, I posted something about enabling mothers on Facebook, which earned me a furious response from another member of the family. It was clear that battle lines had been drawn and I was on the wrong side. I removed, unfriended and blocked them all, but became consumed with their denial of me and my baby.

There is a type of grief so intense that it is akin to madness, and that was the madness that took hold of me. I was powerless to stop it – and didn't want to. These people, Enver and his family, deserved my hate and vitriol. My messages became more and more venomous until eventually I was holding nothing back. I spewed my pain at them unedited, uncensored.

"Do you have any idea of the HELL I'm going through? Do you really not care AT ALL???

SHAME ON YOU. YOU ARE DISGUSTING.

There's a special place in hell for people like you.

You people are EVIL. I hope you live the rest of your lives in HELL."

One day, unable to stop myself, I hacked my way into Enver's long-redundant Facebook account and continued my verbal assault before a wider audience, until a mutual friend spotted what I'd done and urged me to stop. "It's hurting you more than it's hurting them." And she was right. Not once did any of it make me feel better, and their response continued to be to ignore me. Sometimes I thought it would be easier if they told me outright to fuck off, but their silence was so much more effective. To them, it appeared, I, *we*, simply didn't exist.

My time overseas has, to a degree, the desired effect of putting distance between me and the madness. While I've been away, the anger hasn't seemed as pronounced, but the second I touch back down in Cape Town it returns as blind rage. It's as if it's been sitting, waiting for me on the runway ever since I left. I haven't even unclicked my seatbelt and it's there, like the very worst heartburn. It feels like my insides are on fire.

I allow all the other passengers to disembark, while I sit, a hand absentmindedly but protectively across my belly, staring out angrily on to the tarmac. Enver's disappearance and his family's refusal to acknowledge me and the baby have meant there's been no outlet for my anger. Nowhere to vent my spleen. All the rage and venom and hatred, all of it is being internalised, turned inward and, worse, absorbed by the baby. It's *that* thought that tips me over the edge.

As soon as the Uber drops me back home at Sheila's, I grab my car keys from my dressing table and head straight back out the door.

I drive, too fast, the 15 minutes to Enver's mother's house and bang furiously on the front door. When she answers, I want to tell her about my pain and how it feels to have been cast aside, to be unseen, not just by Enver but by *everyone*. I want to appeal to her to put herself in my shoes, as someone facing motherhood for the first time, completely alone and frightened. I want to speak to her, mother to mother, human being to human being, but I can't allow myself that level of vulnerability with this woman, so instead I say, "I can't take care of this baby on my own."

"I don't have any money," she replies. Then, realising that I'm seething, says, "Come in." It's not an invitation; it's a plea not to air the laundry her son has dirtied right there on the stoep within earshot of the neighbourhood curtain twitchers. I follow her inside.

I've rehearsed this moment so many times. Not just in my head but out loud too, grimacing into the mirror or raging in my car. But now, in the moment, I can't find the words, so instead I go on the attack.

"How do you sleep at night?" I demand.

"I sleep very well."

"How, how do you not care?" I counter incredulously.

"I've got my own problems," she sighs. And she does. Addiction has caused chaos and crisis in *her* life too, for years and years. Enver is not the only one of her children whose addiction to heroin has put her nerves on edge and thinned her hair and probably made her ask where *she* herself went so wrong as a mother.

But, just as she hasn't the capacity for mine, I don't have room for her pain or her "problems", and for five minutes the very

144

worst of me erupts and I rage and swear at this woman while a piece of her grows inside me. I don't cry. Not until I get back in the car and drive home. Then the tears come. So many that I have to pull over to the side of the road and let them fall.

I enter my final trimester feeling more alone that I have ever believed possible. After the fight with my own mother at the airport and my outburst at Enver's mother, it's as if the final sentient part of me just switches off. As if my brain knows that for my own protection, my own survival (maybe more so for the survival of the baby), it must immediately block anything that has the potential to trigger my psychological pain receptors that twitch and throb constantly in anticipation of the next strike. Without the release of death, I simply have no more tolerance for pain. Soon it'll only really be the baby that's living, I think. Every day, *I* cease to exist a little more, while every day *she* becomes more vital. Some days I wonder whether her tiny heart isn't actually beating for the both of us.

I'm six weeks away from my due date and unpacking boxes of new crockery and cutlery at the new house when my phone rings.

"Hello?"

"Hello, sis."

It's Thabiso, my brother. Technically, my half-brother, but since being reunited with my biological father and my three siblings almost two years ago, following the release of *Killing Karoline*, there's no "half" anything. They are my family. Thabiso and I have become close, despite the years of siblinghood we've missed out on.

"How's it going?" he asks.

I want to say fine, I want to keep holding it together, but instead I slide down onto the floor of the kitchen of a house I don't ever want to live in, and I cry. I cry until there's nothing left and I'm just whimpering down the phone.

145

"What can I do?" he says.

"Come," I say. "Can you come and be with me when the baby's born?"

"I can," he says. And he does. Because that's what family do.

16

Blood is thicker than water

December 2017, Cape Town

"Hello, you don't know me, but I need to ask you a question. Did you work at the Balalaika in the 1970s?"

The faceless voice on the other end of the line says no.

"The Balalaika Hotel? In Sandown? You never worked there?"

A few muttered uhmmms and ahhs.

"Sir, please, I need to know, did you work at the Balalaika about 40 years ago?"

I'm about to hang up when the voice says, "Yes, but not for very long."

I almost drop the phone.

"When? When did you work there?" I demand. I'm spitting the words out like gunfire, urgent bullets, peppering the ether between us.

The voice doesn't know this about me yet, but these days I'm a straight talker and hate ambiguity.

"I think '77, no '78, uhmmm, sometime like that," comes the reply.

My hands are trembling, and I have to remind myself to breathe. In. Out. Inhale. Exhale.

"Oh my God," I say to myself, but also into the mouthpiece of the phone.

My legs have buckled and brought me to sitting, perched on the edge of the bed.

"Did you have a relationship with a white woman when you worked at the Balalaika?"

"Uhmm … what do you mean a relationship?"

This makes me angry. I've come too far to be fucked around by semantics.

"Sex!" I shout. "Did you have sex with a white woman when you were working at the Balalaika?"

He's muttering, plus the line is bad, like he's speaking to me from 37 years in the past.

I try again.

"Did you know a woman, a woman called Kris? She also worked at the Balalaika?" I'm sounding desperate now.

"Aah," he says. "Kris. That's right. Kris." He's answering me but really I know he's recalling, remembering. Realising.

On the other end of the line, he has been brought to his knees.

This is it.

Thirty. Seven. Years.

"I'm your daughter."

"Oh shit," comes the reply.

Oh shit, indeed.

The thing about killing someone and telling everyone they're dead is that you've got to make sure as shit they really are dead. If you don't, then you have to be prepared for the prospect that they could come back and, if and when they *do*, they're going to want answers. They're also likely to be pretty pissed. In September 1980, when my biological mother clicked her safety belt into its holster and stowed her tray table for take-off back to South Africa for the performance of a lifetime, she had perhaps not given much thought to this.

It is a uniquely peculiar position to occupy, being one who

is *not* dead but alive and vivid and real, experiencing all the extremes of human existence and emotion, and knowing that there are people for whom you exist only as a ghost.

While the weeks, months and years made strangers of my biological mother and I, she seemed to have convinced herself that I *had* died (perhaps her only way of coping) and that I would have the decency to stay dead. But I didn't, and on my 37th birthday I gave birth to something of my own, a book, *Killing Karoline*, which exposed her lie that I had died as a baby. For me, though, the book was less about death and more about rebirth. Writing it allowed me to rewrite myself back to life.

It had taken years since I'd first started jotting down parts of my story in rehab before *Killing Karoline* was ready to be brought into the world. My publisher once described the process as being like a midwife delivering a reluctant baby. There were many moments while writing that I almost buried myself (and my story) again. On these occasions, she would tell me to "write as if they are dead". And so I did. These days I *live* as if they're dead too.

My maternal "family" was horrified by the book and how it exposed their lies. Somehow, they seemed to feel *entitled* to my silence. They were entirely unable to appreciate the psychological impact of being seen as their dirty little secret my whole life.

After meeting my maternal half-brother and his family some years before the book came out, the extended "family" I naively thought I could assimilate into have once again become strangers. A few remained close by long enough to see *Karoline* hit the shelves (maybe to check whether they had earned a mention within its pages), but after that I never saw or heard from them again. It's better that way. Giving birth to *Killing Karoline* helped me to unburden some of the shame I had been carrying around for years and which, crucially, as I would learn in therapy, did not belong to me.

One day, after the book had been out for a couple of years, I came across a review online that read:

This comes as a huge shock and has really affected me. I knew baby Karoline and cradled her in my arms at three weeks. Hoped for a miracle treatment in the UK and mourned her passing for her "devastated" parents. Her mother never seemed to get over it. Now I understand why.

Initially, I found it quite eerie, as if whoever had written it was speaking to the dead. Then I found it sad, and after some time, I found it comforting that here was someone who had borne witness to my young life (and death) before adoption had made me someone else.

One of the most remarkable things to emerge from writing the book was that it led to me meeting my biological father. "You will never know more about him than you do now," my biological mother had told me in a letter almost 20 years before. And with that, for so long and because I thought I had no choice, I had had to be satisfied.

For 37 years, all I had known about my father was what the adoption worker had scrawled in her spidery hand on an A4 sheet of paper titled INFORMATION ON NATURAL FATHER, which had been presented to my adoptive parents when they came to collect me. That's all I apparently deserved to know about the man who made my skin black and put the gap between my two front teeth.

Under NAME was the name people – *white* people – used (and still use) because they would never have bothered to try to pronounce the name given to him by his mother. I have often wondered whether my biological mother ever knew his real name. Did she even realise that the name she breathed and moaned in their forbidden moments together, the name she held on her tongue when she still *tasted* him in her mouth at night, laying and lying next to her husband, was not really his?

Under date of birth was the number 30. His age, presumably, but my father was in fact just 23 years old when I was born. They were both so, *so* young. Where the father's address should have been was scrawled instead "Sotho tribe" (which, prior to coming back to South Africa, I pronounced *soth-oh*) and under nationality it said "Black". Under NOTES ON HEALTH, the social worker had written "appeared fit and no problems known in family". Religion, marital status and other children had been left blank.

I've tried, many times, to picture my biological mother as she answered these questions. Was she guarded? Resigned? Matter-of-fact? Was she as forthcoming as she could be, knowing that this information would one day be imparted to a young woman, desperate for knowledge about who she was and where she came from? Was she, maybe, embarrassed because she knew too little about my father or self-conscious that she perhaps knew too much to claim that theirs had been no more than a one-night tryst? And where was her husband as she answered the questions being posed to her about the black man who'd fathered her black baby? And where was I? Where was I in all of this?

Fairly early on in the writing of *Killing Karoline*, I decided that I would not reveal the real names of certain individuals who appeared in the book. I especially did not want to reveal the true name of my biological father. First, I didn't know whether I could deal with another rejection. The reaction I'd got from my biological mother when I'd reached out to her in my early twenties had done a real number on me. Second, as far as I knew, my biological father was still married and I didn't want to be accused of upsetting yet another family. Lastly – and, in a way, it's not especially easy to articulate – I had always felt protective of my father. Perhaps because of the politics at play during the time he knew my mother. The regime under which they lived served to emasculate, dehumanise and potentially criminalise *him*. The jeopardy of their liaison was so much greater for him than it was for her.

I had thought about my father often over the years. Sometimes, the not knowing became so all-consuming that I thought it might crush me from the inside. There were so many times when, without warning, I would be struck by a compulsion to find out who the hell I really was, and who I could have been, as it related to the man I'd only ever seen as a side profile in an old photograph from the bad old days.

When these moments crept up on me, rudely and seemingly out of nowhere, I would find myself distracted, frantically typing variations of his name into Google, praying that an unpaid parking fine or even a death notice placed by a grieving relative would connect me to the missing jigsaw piece.

When I moved to Johannesburg in 2013, it dawned on me that I could walk past my own father in the street, stand toe to heel behind him in the queue at the bank or sit shoulder to shoulder with him in a taxi, and I would never even know it. I began to look at all black men of a certain age with an easily misinterpreted longing.

My last resort was to reach out to a private investigation firm, the type that can trace a cheating spouse, a deadbeat dad in arrears for *papgeld* or a missing person. My father wasn't exactly missing, but I did want to find him. I contacted three or four different PIs, but the answer was always the same: without an ID number or at least a date of birth, it would be like finding a needle in a haystack. Save your money and forget about the past, one of them told me.

Five months after *Killing Karoline* was released, and with the book garnering considerable media attention, a colleague at the radio station invited me to join him on air for an interview. Koketso and I had become friends during our time together at the station, often sitting out on the balcony in the evening ahead of our respective night-time shows, smoking and shooting the shit. He knew how much it would mean to me to have clarity or, if it had to be, *closure* when it came to my biological father.

Towards the end of the interview, during a commercial break, he leant across the desk towards me.

"Sis," he said, "are we gonna do this?"

I needed someone to push me over the edge and stop letting fear keep me in a state of paralysis.

I sat for a while, contemplating the enormity of what we were about to do.

"Ten seconds," said the engineer driving the studio desk controls.

"Okay," I said, "let's do it." Three, two, one … going live.

Koketso: I had an expectation of a chapter where you're in Mamelodi, Atteridgeville, Soweto, for that matter, and you meet him.

SJ: I wish … It has come to a point now where the need to know my biological father is so strong, it's overwhelming …

Koketso: So, what is his name?

SJ: *long pause* His name is …

And just like that, it was out there.

17

Dackson's daughter

For many years, in the moments when I would look back on my life, what always stood out for me was the number of times I was genuinely surprised by my own reflection. In a shop front or a car window, in the scratched lenses of a passing stranger's Aviators, in the polished cherrywood surface of a café table dusted with never-made-it-into-the-latté granules of Canderel. Times without number, I was startled to see a *whole* person staring back at me, because *inside* I always felt incomplete.

For a long time, the version of me I carried in my head was a very different one from the reflections I was abruptly confronted with in those shiny veneers. In my mind, I was taller, less hunched, my face showing no signs of the battles I'd won and the wars I'd lost. In my head, I still had the physique of my early twenties when, by virtue of starvation, vomiting and laxatives, I'd managed to sculpt myself an impressive set of Nefertiti-like cheekbones, a concave midriff and a visible ribcage. In reality, the difference was a fuck ton of disappointments.

There were times, many, when I'd been completely taken aback when the figure I glimpsed walking in through the automatic doors of a Monday morning *didn't* look like she'd been daubed onto a canvas by an expressionist painter. Then I'd be forced to see how years of my life had been spent making

154

sure my outsides didn't match my insides. Inventing versions of myself for glass and gloss and gleam.

Occasionally, though, there were moments in which my reflection mirrored how I saw myself in my mind's eye. I looked like someone who had forgotten to inhabit their body. As if I'd woken up and bypassed the closet where Sara-Jayne was draped on a wire hanger waiting to be pulled on. I looked stark and raw and missing. I looked like a half a person.

I'm not a morning person. Mornings are heavy, as if doing their best to creep out from under the full weight of the night without letting on what they're doing. It's 04:15am and our flight is at 05:40am. I've ordered an Uber and, while we wait for it to arrive, I'm niggled, as I always am, by the notification that tells me that the payment for the trip has *already* ping-pinged out of my account. So bloody presumptuous. What if he's late? Or rude? Or smelly? Or drunk?

"What if he's late? Or rude? Or smelly? Or drunk?"

"Your dad?" asks Enver on an in-breath. He's pulling on the remainder of the cigarette I've just handed him. He always does that, tells me to "Keep me a *skyf*", as if by only having the last dregs and drag of my cigarettes he's not really having one and therefore can't really be deemed to be taking more of my stuff without paying *for* or paying *back* or contributing *anything*.

"The Uber driver," I say without looking up from my phone.

Enver and I are flying to Johannesburg to meet my biological father, Dackson. It's been 10 days since I asked for the public's help in finding him. It's been a week since he and I first spoke on the phone. I still can't quite believe it's really happening. Within two days of the radio interview with Koketso, I'd received a message on Facebook. It was from a woman in Limpopo who was a member of a group called Waar in die Wêreld (Where in the World), for people trying to trace long-lost friends and

155

family members. She had seen my plea for information and, without introduction, emotion or fanfare, had sent me a message containing details that would minutes later connect me with the man who gave me my smile.

His reaction, after his initial shock, floored me. "How *are* you?" he asked. I was completely taken aback. I'd buffed up my emotional armour for the prospect of another disappointment, another *rejection*, like the one I'd experienced years before from his former lover, my biological mother. But, instead, he'd been full of questions. All about my life. Who were the people who raised me? Were they good parents? Had I had a good life? Was I happy?

They were questions I wanted to answer, but I didn't know how. How does one summarise 37 years into three minutes of airtime remaining? It's a lot to tell a man you've never met but who is also your father, in your first-*ever* conversation, over the *phone*, and so I'd just keep saying, "I'm fine, I'm fine," over and over again. There was, however, one question I *could* answer. "Can I see you?" And, of course, the answer had been an unequivocal "yes".

I watch the image of a car left-turn, right-turn its way through the crisscross of lines on my phone screen. It looks like a computer game from the eighties. The car is apparently being driven by someone called Innocent, but the twinkle in his eye that stares out from his profile picture suggests he is anything but. The clock display reads 04:20am. Innocent and his computer car are apparently two minutes away. I'm tapping my foot anxiously, but then remember that I'm already 37 years late.

Ignoring my disapproving tut, Enver flicks the cigarette butt over the wall and onto the pavement. I pull another smoke from the box, already half-empty and poking out from the zip pocket on the front of my handbag.

"Don't light another one," he says, as if the decision about when, why and how many of the cigarettes *I* work hard to pay for and smoke is any his business.

I feel the familiar flicker of irritation licking at that raw spot behind my heart, but I tap the cigarette back into its spot in the box.

Another notification tells me Innocent has arrived and, looking over the wall, I see a tall, Zimbabwean-looking guy heaving himself out of the driver's seat of a white Toyota Corolla. I give a smile and a wave and Enver carries our bags down the steps to Innocent and his waiting car.

We'd packed last night. Me far too much for four days in my trusty black carry-on case designed specifically for short domestic trips like the one we're about to take. I've lost count of the adventures this case and I have been on. Up in the air and down on the ground. Kuala Lumpur, London, Bangkok, Vegas and, today, back to Joburg.

Enver doesn't have a case. He has a bag, an old holdall presented to him by his mother yesterday when we'd announced we were flying to Jozi to meet my biological father. She'd seemed keen to point out this was a loan, not a gift.

"To the airport?" confirms Innocent once we're all in.

I nod.

"Yes, please, buddy," says Enver, patting the back of Innocent's seat, like he's somehow running the show.

I look across at him: clean T-shirt, beard trimmed, hair slicked and styled with my expensive anti-frizz pomade. At least he's in a good mood, I think to myself and once again feel grateful for having him.

I slink back into the seat and fidget until the back of my neck rests just so on the headrest. I reach out my hand and place it on Enver's thigh. He turns just his head to look at me and smiles.

I don't realise, as we pull away, that I'll not return to the house the same person I am right now in this moment. I also don't realise that there is four days' supply of methadone decanted into an old cough-medicine bottle and tucked into the inside pocket of the borrowed holdall.

At the airport I buy us coffee that tastes and smells like leather and, slaves to the nicotine that we are, we stand outside and puff away under a sign that clearly states "No Smoking" while working out how long it'll be once we're through Departures before we can light up again. Fucking addicts. Every so often I whip out my phone and do a Facebook Live or other such social-media intrusion into the lives of people who have probably followed me on a whim but are now wondering where the unfollow button is.

A friend has urged me to record every moment of the meeting for posterity, but for me it's about much more than that. I have a need for people to see that this is happening, as if to prove to them that I am wanted in the place nature had created and intended me to be. That, actually, there *was* nothing so wrong with me or unlovable about me that the person who carried me for nine months should be unwilling to nurture me as the stars had written it and the oceans had commanded. More, that my being accepted by Dackson, my *father*, has nothing to do with anything I might offer him, any hole in the soul that needs filling, any gaping wound left by the tragedy of infertility, but simply because I am his daughter.

When, in my early twenties, I began to develop a natural curiosity about where I came from, I was received by my biological mother, not with open arms – as far too many made-for-TV movies would have us believe – but rather with horror and outrage. "Can't we sue?" she had asked the social worker at the adoption agency who had reached out to her on my behalf. Even her latest husband, a bankable American, had been ready to pay to make it, make *me*, go away, back into the grave his wife had dug for me all those years ago.

In case I hadn't got the message, my maternal grandmother had written me a letter to let me know in no uncertain terms that I was *persona non grata*: "*Cease trying to get in touch with my eldest daughter ... Never contact our family again.*"

A few years later, when *Killing Karoline* came out, they were all, predictably, horrified and outraged about that too.

At the time, I did my best to shrug it off, rolling my eyes at their rejection of me and the lengths to which they were prepared to go to keep the "dead baby" lie alive. But it *did* affect me, deeply. It was inexplicably painful and almost impossible not to take on. "It's not about you, it's entirely a reflection of them," my therapist would say, but believing that was easier said than done. I couldn't understand the lengths they were prepared to go to keep their awful secret, when there was now no reason for it. So, when Dackson had not only *not* slammed the phone down, but also asked when we could meet, I was staggered.

We have agreed to meet at a café inside a mall in Johannesburg's affluent North. Me, Enver and Shaun, an old friend from my Joburg rehab days, arrive an hour beforehand. I need time to get myself together. I realise I have no idea what he looks like. I have just one photograph of him. Taken during the bad old days. My biological mother had sent it to the adoption agency years before. The picture, tellingly, was one she'd kept for years in an album of her time at the hotel where they worked. It's of a white woman (not her) standing with four black staff members, three men and a woman. She hadn't indicated which of the men was Dackson, but a general consensus among several of my friends identified him as "second from the left".

It's a profile shot, revealing only the side of his face, but it's clear from that alone that this is my father. How much does a person change in nearly 40 years, I wonder, thinking not necessarily of him.

When the moment finally comes, it is remarkable and heartbreaking and life-changing. My father pulls me to him and sobs, "My daughter! My daughter!" For that moment nothing those other people, my biological mother and her family, have ever said – or haven't said – matters. We are, all of us, crying. Enver, using my phone to film everything, has tears streaming down his face. Releasing me from his arms, my father grips my hands and looks directly into my eyes. He smiles and I notice the gap between his two front teeth. I smile my own back at him. When his two sons and daughter, my brothers and my sister, arrive later, we will all smile our same smile, given to us by our late grandmother.

"How does it feel to meet your daughter for the first time, sir?" asks Shaun, when we are finally seated around two small round tables pulled together to create one.

"The first time? No, this is not the first time. I saw her when she was a baby, a few days old. Her mother brought her to the hotel to show me." I am dumbstruck.

"You were wrapped up in blankets. It was August, it was cold," he says, bending his arm as if holding a baby. "She said to me, look," he gestures his bent arm towards us, pulling us into history, "and I took one look at you and said, that child is a Makwala."

It is the single most profound moment of my life.

On the plane home four days later, while Enver sleeps, I catch my breath and recall, moment by moment, the events of the last couple of weeks. I watch the video he has captured of the meeting, reliving it frame by frame. How incredible it is, I think, that while my father and I were being reunited after decades as strangers, in the background, like extras in a movie, people continued moving through their Saturday-afternoon lives, completely unaware that at the same time someone lost was being found.

Meeting my father feels like the beginning of the end of a life I've lived as an incomplete person. A book in which the first chapter, having been ripped from the spine, leaves the reader and the characters unsure of who they are right from the start.

There's a misconception that adoption reunions are "happy endings". It's a simplification that doesn't allow for the trauma of relinquishment and the grief and loss of estrangement. It's a feeling almost impossible to describe to people who are not adopted. It's like a cavernous black hole, the feeling of something perpetually missing. For me, the years of not knowing had created something akin to a tumour, which, if left untreated, would grow to the point that it would eventually push me out of myself.

We touch down in Cape Town and I am not the same person who left four days before. I am convinced that meeting my father is the missing piece of the puzzle. What more could there possibly be? Finally, I will be healed and delivered from the malady that has plagued me my whole life. I don't yet understand that the meeting is just one step towards the healing and not the healing itself.

Part II

Part II

18

Zora

Your daughter is being born tomorrow.

Send.

Another message to his mother's phone that will likely remain unopened and unanswered, but the only one out of the dozens I've sent over the last six months that will matter, ultimately.

The baby isn't due for another nine days, but since my feet are now swollen beyond recognition and my blood pressure is approaching overweight, diabetic smoker levels, Dr Wondimu has suggested we "get this show on the road" and induce.

I'm all for it. For months the terror of impending single-motherhood has routinely trumped the discomfort of pregnancy, but finally, in a twist I never saw coming, I want this baby out of me more than I want to avoid the inevitable chaos and heartache of solo parenting. There's also a resignedness to my situation that has previously eluded me. The baby is coming. Enver is gone. It is what it is. What is happening is happening, with nothing to be done except *let* it happen. I wouldn't go so far as to call it acceptance, but it's as close as dammit.

Inducing also takes away the element of surprise, which, once upon a time (*before* I was pregnant), had seemed so exciting and delightfully made-for-TV-movie-esque, but which right now is just the level of unpredictable I can do without. We'd tried to schedule my brother's arrival and his week-long stay as close to the baby's likely delivery window as possible, but I'd been increasingly worried that she would continue floating contentedly for the duration of his visit and then decide to make her grand entrance in the middle of night when I was home alone. I'd been praying she hadn't inherited her father's sense of catastrophic timing.

We'd all been holding thumbs for the last few weeks that the complex diary configurations, frantic calendar predictions and desperate finger crossing we'd been doing would be enough when push (or push*ing*) came to shove.

"So, we give her a nudge, yes?" Wondimu had said when I waddled, grumbling and uncomfortable, into his office for the last of my scheduled appointments before my due date. "Yes," I say, "I'm over it" – and I am. I truly don't know how I'm going to survive the next few weeks and months, but the constant peeing, the unrelenting backache and the sense that my own vagina might prolapse into the toilet bowl every time I use the bathroom means I am *very* ready to not be pregnant any more. Also, another surprising but not unwelcome development is that I am now genuinely intrigued, excited even, to meet this little creature who has been wreaking havoc on my back and bladder for the last few months.

"So, when do you want to do this?" asks Wondimu, "Tomorrow? We can do it tomorrow?" He's looking at the calendar on his desktop. Suddenly, despite having had almost nine months to get used the idea of a baby, it hits me properly that once she's out, she's out and everything changes. Forever. I've been so busy getting the practical things ready for her arrival over the last few weeks that I've failed to really acknowledge the departure my own life is about to make.

For most of my adult life I've done entirely as I've pleased. Moving through life unburdened and unencumbered. Making decisions, the consequences of which, good or bad, have been mine alone to bear. On a whim I've moved house, city, country, continent, sometimes never knowing where I'm headed until I've arrived. I've bungeed off the highest of bridges and swum carefree and carelessly in deep, black oceans without concern that I might not bounce back or resurface. For years, although I haven't realised it, I've been living in the "before". As soon as the baby is here, I'll have moved into the after, and nothing will ever be the same again.

"Uhmm, no, not tomorrow. C-can we do the day after rather?" As much as I like Dr Wondimu, I don't want to tell him that I need one last night of uninterrupted sleep, one more recklessly fast cruise down the highway wearing my bad-girl Aviators and pumping Blaklez or YoungstaCPT at full volume, one more day being just me. I'm too embarrassed to tell him all this, but he's been around the block long enough to see it written all over my face.

"The day after tomorrow? Sure," he says. "Whatever you want. You come early, the day after tomorrow, and we'll have a baby." I leave the hospital, once again thanking the universe for Dr Wondimu.

Before I drive out of the car park, I take my phone out of my bag and type,

Your daughter is being born tomorrow.

I hit Send.

The next morning, I braid my hair, paint my nails and repack my hospital bag for the hundredth time. In go the breast pads, the nipple cream and the pack of enormous, post-delivery maternity pads my pregnancy app has told me are a must-have. In goes the new, and now I come to see it, rather inappropriately sexy nightdress I'd bought to allow for easy breast-feeding, and in go the pair of warm fluffy socks I'd had to ferret around at the bottom of my winter clothes box to find. In (and out again) go my favourite perfume, and three, then four, then two small bottles of mineral water. Lastly, in goes the pink-and-gold striped babygro.

In the late afternoon, Thabiso and I take a drive. City-dweller that he is, he wants to see the ocean. It's a beautiful day and Cape Town is showing off. At the beach the first of the season's tourists are simultaneously acquiring melanomas and sipping Instagrammable bubbles. We park and make our way down to the water's edge. Fire sign be damned, I love the ocean and blissfully saunter straight in. I wish I had the beach all to myself. I'd strip naked and wade further and further in until I was fully submerged, then I'd float on back, my huge belly up to the sun, a big brown whale.

From the sand, Thabiso grins at me while I splash ecstatically in the shallows. The coolness on my swollen feet is blissful. I never want to leave this water, I think.

Just as the sun goes down, we head back to the car and, while I'm awkwardly balancing my bulk against the front bumper and trying to brush the sand from between my toes, my phone rings.

"Hello?"

"Hi, my baby."

"Hello?"

"Hi."

"Who is this?

"It's me."

It's him. A day late and a dollar short, but it's him. Immediately I start to cry. Six months of shock, hurt, betrayal, abandonment, terror, rage, worry, loneliness, but the overwhelming feeling is actually one of relief.

"It's okay, it's okay, baby," he coos at the end of the line.

"Where are you?"

"Where are you?"

"In town."

"At the beach."

After six months, this pedestrian back and forth is all we can manage?

"How are you, my baby?"

Six months of silence. And now it's "my baby"? I snap back to reality.

"Listen here," I say, my mouth stuffed full of everything he's left me to carry on my own. "I'm giving you a 24-hour pass to be present for the birth of your daughter. After that, you can fuck off back to the rock you've been living under." I need Enver to know that I'm not the same person I was a whole-fucking-half-year-ago.

"I mean it, Enver. I don't want to talk about anything, nothing. I'm not doing this for me and I'm not a fuck doing it for you. I couldn't care if you dropped dead tomorrow. I'm doing this for her, so that one day, if nothing else, when she asks – and she will ask, Enver – I'll be able to tell her that her father witnessed her entry into the world."

"Okay. Okay. Thank you. I'll be there. Thank you."

"We need to be at the hospital at 07:30am. I'll pick you up at 7am. Be ready."

"I will."

When I arrive outside his mother's house almost 12 hours later, all I can think is that he looks the same. Although his hair is longer, his beard too. It's coarse and unkempt like steel wool and there are significantly more greys than there were six months ago. Six months.

He's also darker. I've never seen him this dark. Like dirt. Particularly his forehead, and the back of his neck. The part where once upon a time I would draw my tongue all the way along from his collarbone and he'd instantly get hard.

I've pulled up a few metres away from the house, and I'm watching him striding towards the car with that all-too-familiar gait. Denial prevents me from looking too hard or too long. I know that if I do, I'm in danger of seeing what's really there. So I decide he looks the same and make myself believe it. But, if we were to compare two photographs side by side, one from the "good old days" and one from now, I wouldn't be able to deny it. He looks like – no, he *is* – a smack-ravaged street junkie.

He's wearing a flannel shirt I've never seen before, cobalt-blue-and-green checks, which, like everything else he has on, is swallowing him whole. Two of the buttons are missing and there are bleach spots bleeding onto one of the cuffs. Why only one of them? It's early November, approaching the start of summer, but it's early and overcast and threatening to rain – too cold for the flip-flops he's almost wearing. His cracked heels trespass over the edge of the soles. His toenails are blue-black. It doesn't even occur to me why he wouldn't wear something else, a different, more suitable type of shoe. I'm wearing flip-flops too, but that's because my feet simply won't be persuaded into anything else.

"Let me look at you," he says, grinning to reveal teeth that now look too big in his head. Like a horse's teeth, long and brown and ready to bite.

I say nothing but shift my enormous weight exhaustedly from left buttock to right.

"Can I have a hug?" he says.

This can't be real. *Any* of it.

"No."

"Can I touch your belly?"

"No."

"Okay then." He's trying to be contrite but there's an edge to his voice. It can't *possibly* be resentment?

"New car?" he says, checking out the mommy wagon for which I traded my sporty two-door in several weeks ago.

"I guess."

"It's nice."

"It's necessary. I'm having a baby. The other one was too small."

"Shall I drive?"

No, I say again, still staring straight ahead. I know what he's trying to do, and part of me wants to go along with it. We drive for about a minute, neither of us saying a word, and then he breaks the terrible silence.

"SJ," he sighs, "we have a problem."

I keep my eyes on the road while he twists in the passenger seat to face me. I want to turn the radio on, but now, all of sudden, there's too much noise in the car.

"SJ!" he says again, as if somehow I hadn't heard him the first time.

I inhale loudly and dramatically: "*We* don't have a problem, Enver – *you* have a problem."

"Please. Please just turn here and stop ... over there," he pleads, pointing to a road up ahead.

I sigh, but I do it because I know he won't make it if I don't. If I don't stop and let him out of the car to go score, he won't make it through the birth of our daughter. The insanity of it all leads me to a spontaneous, derisive snort, which earns me a look of complete bewilderment.

He hops out of the car.

"Five minutes. I'll be five minutes."

I don't look to see which way he goes, as if to do so would be to acknowledge the horror and fucked-up-ness of what's happening. Fifteen minutes later he slides back into the car. We arrive at the hospital late, just before 8am.

Reception is being manned by a pretty, youngish-looking woman with a shoulder-length bob and an abrupt fringe.

"And how can we help you today?"

"I'm here to have a baby," I say wearily.

171

A baby. Not my baby and certainly not his baby.

"Okay," she smiles. "Take a seat just here. And I'll need to you complete these ..." She pushes several forms across the desk for me to fill in.

I lower myself ungraciously into the chair and start writing.

"What's the date?"

"The sixth," says the woman behind the desk.

"Yeah, the sixth," parrots Enver unnecessarily. I can feel that he's desperately trying to be part of this, to be relevant, and it makes me mad and sad all at once.

"Wednesday," he adds unhelpfully.

"Wednesday's child is full of woe," I mumble to no one.

I pass the forms back across the desk and try to pay attention as the fringe explains how to get to the maternity ward. I attempt to haul myself out of the chair and, seeing me struggling, Enver leaps up to offer a supportive arm. I don't want his help, but nor do I want to give birth in a gauche faux-velvet wingback in the reception area of the hospital.

It's only when I reluctantly take his bony arm to heave myself to standing that I notice that he's no longer wearing the blue-and-green checked shirt. He's literally sold the shirt off his back.

In the maternity ward we're shown to my (mercifully private) room where I change into my nightdress and position myself as comfortably as I can on the bed. Enver darts around in a pantomime of attentiveness, fluffing pillows, pouring me water and asking me if I'm comfortable – which, of course, I'm not, because I'm nine months pregnant, but *because* I'm nine months pregnant and physically and emotionally spent, and also because I'm just few hours away from pushing an actual human out of my body, I let him.

It strikes me as extraordinary that, even after everything, we're able to slip back into this dance of familiarity, even fondness. On the one hand, it feels deeply comforting; on the other, it horrifies me. It's so contrary to the anguish his disappearance has caused in the last few months I've been carrying his child.

I watch him delve into my bag and take out some lotion. He pulls up a chair at the side of the bed and lifts my feet onto his lap and presses his fingers into my soles. Again, the intimacy of it both soothes and sickens me. I look at the back of his head and wonder, with a sense of disquiet, how it is that two Envers can exist in the same space and time simultaneously. The devil and the doting partner.

We've been in the room a little over an hour when Dr Wondimu arrives. As the door opens, I catch a glimpse of Enver, quick enough to see a shadow of shame cast itself over his gaunt face. Maybe it's because I'm drunk in my relief that he's here and that I won't have to do this on my own, and that, for what it's worth, my daughter will know that her father was present (in body, if not mind) when she was born, but *I* still can't see just *how* bad Enver looks. He looks terrible. And he knows it. As though he's been sleeping on the street for weeks. Which, I'll learn later, he has.

Wondimu's face lights up with what appears to be genuine pleasure when he spots Enver "Ah, Mr King, Mr King, it's *good* to see you!" he shakes his hand enthusiastically. He's too decent and too professional to dream of asking where Enver has been or to make him feel anything other than a part of the next few hours and our daughter's entrance into the world. If Enver is the villain of the piece, Dr Wondimu is the hero.

A few hours later, with Enver gripping my hand and stroking my forehead, our daughter, Zora, is born. Enver nervously cuts the chord and watches, his eyes wide, as they weigh and check her over. She is swaddled and placed in her father's arms where he beams into her beautiful, wrinkled little face. I can't take my eyes off them. We are wheeled back to the room and, with me in the bed, the baby in her cot and Enver curled into a chair in a corner of the room, we fall asleep. The three of us.

By the time morning creeps in through the curtains, it becomes clear that there's been a shift change. Attentive, beaming Enver has left and been replaced by agitated, pacing, clucking-for-a-fix Enver. I'm beginning to see just how bad things are. It's like being in a room with an angry stranger. When he'd first told me he was using, all that time ago in Jimmy's living room, what had played on my mind afterwards, to the point of delirium, was *how* I couldn't have seen it. How can you live with a heroin addict in full-blown addiction and not know? What's becoming obvious is that Enver's using is now no longer about getting high; he needs a fix just to be able to *function*. Brown is now his lifeblood. It means more to him than anything else in the world.

Without even acknowledging his newborn daughter feeding on my breast, he begins his patter. "C-Can I borrow some money? I'll pay you back." Pay me back? Does he think I've forgotten that less than 24 hours ago he sold one of the four items of clothing he owns so he could score? I'm suddenly reminded of the time at the train station years before when he'd asked me for money. It was so long ago. And this time there's no smiling blonde to help him out.

"I'm not giving you money for heroin, Enver," I say through gritted teeth. His face darkens. It frightens me how quickly he shifts between characters.

"Then I'll just have to go and steal something!" He's clutching. Desperate.

How is this *happening*? How is this my life and the life of my day-old baby? I'm a terrible mother.

As Enver switches back to pleading, my phone rings. It's Mel, a friend of ours, calling for a baby update. Mel is also a recovering addict with 20 years clean time under her belt. Smack was also her drug of choice. I tell her what's happening.

"Just give it to him," she sighs. "I know it's awful, but give it to him, because you need him right now and the fact is he's not capable of doing this *without* using."

I press my cheek against Zora's downy scalp and start to cry. She's right. I do need him; the last six months has left me completely broken. At this point, I need to do what I can to survive. I reach into the bedside cabinet and fish R50 out of my bag. I see the relief flood into his face when I press it into his hands and I nearly vomit.

A little over an hour later, he walks back in while I'm feeding Zora. I *hate* myself for being pleased to see him. Doting father again, he takes Z and gently burps her on his shoulder, changes her nappy, swaddles her in a blanket and rocks her back to sleep on his arm. He leaves twice more before the day is out; the last time he's back within a few minutes.

"I managed to find somewhere to go at the back of the hospital," he explains casually, as if he's telling me he's been able to find a more convenient parking spot. Z is asleep in the cot next to me, else I'd scream until I was hoarse that he's fucking despicable and ruining what should be the most precious time of our lives. Instead I settle for "Good for you".

Three days after Zora is born, the three of us leave the hospital. With Enver at the wheel, we drive home.

19

A house is not a home

The pain is not nearly as bad as they said it would be. Nine days after having Zora, I'm moving around easily and, even though I'm still swollen, like a partially deflated bagpipe, I'm no longer shuffling tentatively along like I had in the hospital. It's discomfort more than pain. Like a cramp. If I laugh, it feels like someone is twanging a large, taut rubber band lodged inside me somewhere between my belly button and groin. It's bearable. It will be a few more days before I realise that the pills they handed me as I left the hospital have me jacked to the max and that I, a recovering pill junkie, have been floating around on a codeine high for the better part of a week.

Notwithstanding the fact that Enver had swept back in at the eleventh hour, the pre-birth planning I'd done to ensure I wasn't going to be alone when the baby arrived has paid off. My brother went back to Joburg the afternoon we brought Zora home from the hospital, and my friend arrived from the States a couple of days later. In the short window in between, Enver, Zora and I play house.

For two days, I watch in awe as Enver takes care of Z. I marvel at how comfortable he seems with her. I envy his casual confidence in doing simple things that tend to scare and intimidate me. Things like picking her up out of her bassinet, folding her chubby little arms and legs into her onesies and placing her in her car seat. I am terrified of doing something wrong, or of hurting her. I'm not used to babies. I've spent years avoiding them. I've never even changed a nappy, but Enver, an uncle several times over, seems to take it all in his stride. Sometimes I'll catch him looking at her exactly the way I imagined he would look at our children when, all those years ago, I dreamed we would have a family of our own. It is so confusing, that one who has brought such chaos can also bring such calm. The entire situation is a heartbreaking mindfuck.

Although Enver hasn't asked for any more money since the hospital, he nonetheless still disappears twice a day. He claims he's managed to find someone to sort him out with some methadone, which will keep him straight in lieu of the gear. A combination of post-birth exhaustion and the codeine wave I have inadvertently been riding means I have not been inclined to interrogate him.

With my best friend about to arrive from America, I know it's time to put an end to the madness. I'd initially given Enver 24 hours' access to our lives, and his time is now long up. There is no way, now we've brought Zora home, that I am prepared to fall into a normalising of his using. "You want to do that, you do it at your mother's house," I tell him, standing in my driveway, a protective arm on my gate post, creating a barrier between him and us. (*Us. I am now an "us".*)

"Go and only come back when you're clean and ready to be part of our lives." And, with that, I dramatically slam the gate with an almighty clang that throbs in my temples long after he has gone and the gate latch has smashed back into its holster. Like a scene out of a soap opera. Even I'm convinced that I mean it.

"Only come back when you're clean and ready to be part of our lives." And he *would* come back because, of course, he *does* want to be part of our lives.

177

Ten days before, had he not gripped my hand, his beautiful, deceitful mouth pressed against my forehead while together we watched and wept as our baby, gorgeous and ghastly, was heaved out of my gaping belly? *He* was the one who'd severed the gristly, bloody chord, changed the first milky-shit-filled nappy and rocked her to sleep in the crook of his arm on that first night that we became three. Of course he would come back.

I was even more sure of it when he called me that same evening and told me he'd got hold of some meds that would help him through a detox.

"I can *do* this," he told me. "I'm *going* to do it. I love you guys and I promise I'll see you soon."

That was five days ago, and even though they'd warned me at the hospital not to drive for six weeks, I feel fine. Plus, I'm desperate to see him. I'm desperate for him to see his daughter. To keep her fresh in his mind.

With Zora sleeping in the back of the car, I drive the six minutes to his mother's house. "I'm doing it!" I whisper to her dozing reflection in the rearview mirror. The "it" is all manner of things: it is salvaging something that I desperately want to resemble a family, it is being a mother to a child I never thought I would ever have, it is driving when they told me I shouldn't. I'm a fucking warrior, I tell myself immodestly.

When I arrive, he is waiting, reed thin, leaning on the Vibracrete and eking out the last drags of a cigarette. He expertly flicks it into the road and at the same time propels himself off the wall with the sole of his foot. He starts towards the car and before he opens the door, dips down and looks at Zora in her car seat through the back window. His deadly smile splits his face in two and, for a second, I wonder which version of Enver we will be taking home with us today.

"Shall I drive?" he mouths, nodding in the direction of the steering wheel.

I grin back at him, unable to help myself.

"Yeah," I say and scoot into the passenger seat and let him take control.

Two days later we're playing house. He's stretched out on the sofa, Zora on his chest, watching a documentary about UFOs; I'm sorting through endless pastel-coloured baby clothes and impossibly tiny mittens. I'm looking for something in particular. The babygro I bought the day I felt Zora moving for the first time. During my pregnancy, whenever things threatened to derail me, I'd take it out, drape it across my growing belly and tell myself things were going to be okay. Once or twice I even believed it. Half an hour goes by and still I can't find it. I've turned out the cupboards, my hospital bag and the boot of the car, and upended the laundry basket. After a while, my pacing distracts Enver from the aliens and he asks me what's wrong. I tell him, and when I do, I see his cheek twitch ever so slightly, the way I've seen it do a thousand times. I suddenly think I might pass out, so I lean against the bookcase. A lifetime passes and I exhale slowly.

"Swear to me," I whisper, "swear to me you didn't take it."

"I didn't," he says. "Sara-Jayne, I *swear*."

Before I can stop myself, I say it.

"Swear on her life." I can't stand to look at her as the words spill out and the guilt threatens to take my legs out from under me.

He blinks, then pauses for less than half a second. "I swear," he says, looking me dead in the eye. "On her life."

And, instantly, I know. I know that he has stolen our daughter's clothes to sell for heroin.

179

20

Helping hands

It's a Sunday afternoon and I'm sitting outside a church, in my car, with both breasts exposed. A hungry but fussy two-week-old Zora is unable to choose between one enormous postpartum tit and the other, so I'm manoeuvring her back and forth between the two. Any qualms I ever had about breastfeeding in public or the need to modestly cover up when feeding have been swiftly overcome since becoming an on-demand feeder of this ravenous little creature.

Two weeks into the mom gig and we're still hitting a few bum notes when it comes to feeding. It's hard – really fucking hard – but I'm determined, despite the challenges: that first agonising pull before the let-down, the cracked and leaky nipples. Mercifully, it does seem to be getting easier day by day and I'm surprised to discover that I actually enjoy breastfeeding. There's the bonding factor, of course; I truly love cradling her against me, stroking her perfectly shaped head and inhaling her intoxicating new baby scent, but what I really love about it is that it distracts me from the constant gnawing feeling I have, the one that sits, aching, behind my diaphragm like an ulcer, of being completely fucking useless. Here's something I *can* do, I tell myself. It helps ease some of the guilt and shame I've been piling fastidiously into the ever-expanding "World's Worst Mom" backpack I've been lugging around with me for the last six months.

We are here waiting for Enver who is *inside* the church with a bunch of other addicts slurping cheap coffee and trying not to pick up drugs, *just for today*. I've told him (as I've been telling him for years) that if he's serious about getting clean, he needs to attend the support groups. Now, though, it's a non-negotiable. It's one of the conditions of him being allowed to be part of our lives, which is what he says he wants.

We're also trying to find a rehab centre that will take him, for free, because all my spare cash has gone to setting up the new house and supporting the baby we made, *together,* nine months ago. The fact that he's managed to detox has given me renewed hope, but the revelation (and *eventually* his confession) about the babygro has absolutely floored me. Enver needs intensive help to make sure nothing like that *ever* happens again.

There's a possibility of his getting a space at a Christian-based outreach programme, but the waiting list is long and in the interim we'd be expected to attend church every Sunday. At that, my atheist-leaning hackles went up, but beggars can't be choosers, so we went once to check it out. It had been two hours of handclapping to some inordinately loud and lively praise and worship music and then another hour listening to the high-spirited testimony of an exceedingly well-dressed pastor whose shoes were the pointiest and shiniest I'd ever seen. Enver seemed pretty into it, but I spent most of the time concerned about permanent damage being done to newborn Zora's eardrums. I also couldn't help but wonder what I could sell in order to make a sizeable donation to Pastor What-ever-his-name-was and bump Enver up the waiting list.

And so, until we get some news about a rehab, it's daily meetings. Not an unreasonable request, given the circumstances, and if he's to have any hope of staying clean, meetings like this will have to become his new addiction. He has to start "doing the work" (like I had to do, I frequently remind him) because no one wakes up one morning in the midst of a 20-year heroin addiction and decides they're just going to stop chasing the dragon.

Because Enver's been telling me for so long about his fear of going cold turkey, the fact that he's now *physically* clean means I mistakenly believe that the really hard part is over for him. I've started to believe that the heroin itself is the problem, that the physical addiction is the main thing that must be overcome, the thing standing in the way of the fairy tale I've been writing, directing and starring in for the last 13 years. I've even begun to convince myself that now that the junk is out of his system, everything will be okay. A quick stint in rehab and *alles will be oraait by die huis*. I've completely and conveniently forgotten about the mental obsession of addiction, what so many experts and support programmes call the greater part of the disease. It's almost as if the last 13 years of my own recovery and being surrounded by other addicts have meant absolutely nothing.

I should know better, but instead I tell myself (and Enver) that, having stopped using, all he needs to do is get on with a recovery programme, step up and do the steps, blurt out all his wrongdoings and resentments to (yet another) sponsor and get to work rebuilding that white picket fence I wanted him to erect for us all those years ago when our shoulders brushed in the passageway of the cuckoo's nest. If he doesn't, I tell myself, it can only mean that he doesn't *want* to and that he doesn't love us and that he prefers his life as a skin-and-bone man, skarreling the streets for his next hit, in too-short track pants and worn-out shoes. And that's a possibility I cannot allow myself to entertain.

I'm prepared to do whatever it takes to make it easier for him, because now that he's back in our lives, I've begun believing that the possibility of a happily-ever-after is still within my, our, *my* reach. I just have to create the perfect environment for it, and I, we, *I* will be back on track. If I don't, he might not see the light. If I don't, the drugs will win. If I don't, he could die (which is true). If I don't, then what?

Without invitation, I have appointed myself Enver's line manager in recovery and, in fact, in life too. I think I'm helping. I think I know best. In every single thing he does, I have a suggestion on how he could do it differently, quicker, more thoroughly, better, ultimately more to my liking and comfort. And rather than fight me on it, he should just do it *my* way, because, after all, he owes me because of all he's put me through and all I've done for him.

And so I exhaust myself trying to construct a reality for Enver that makes anything other than total dedication and desire for recovery and a better life – one with me and Z and love and laughter and lemonade – completely unthinkable. All the while I'm also aware of a tiny but persistent voice in the back of my head that's telling me I have to fix this, not for him and for his good, but because I *can't* do it alone. I need him to get this right, because if he doesn't, there is no way I'll survive.

The LCD clock display on the dashboard clicks to 2pm and less than a minute later the doors to the church are flung open and 20 or so addicts are released back into life on life's terms. Most are reaching into their pockets or already stuffing into their mouths and lighting the cigarettes they've been jonesing for for the last hour. I'm scanning, frantically, the heads of the crowd, looking for Enver. Although I saw him go in and have had my eyes trained on the narthex of the church for the last 57 minutes, I wouldn't bet my last on the fact that his will be one of the heads coming back out. He could have snuck out through an Enver-sized window in the bathroom or even a skylight in the pastor's vestibule. Enver's always looking for a back door.

This is who I am now. I'm a watcher. A detective. A keeper. A madwoman.

Soon enough, I spot him and the relief hits deep and soothing, like the first pull on the cigarettes I no longer smoke. He's smiling animatedly with a couple of people. I realise one of them is Jimmy, his old sponsor. I haven't seen Jimmy since that day in his lounge, when I was three months pregnant and the truth came out about Enver's drug-taking. I'm relieved to see him and eager to helpfully suggest to Enver on our drive home that he do whatever is necessary to convince Jimmy to be his sponsor again. Seeing them both walking over to the car, I pluck Z from my breast and rearrange my T-shirt.

"Hello!" I say brightly to Jimmy. He grins back at me wryly.

"How was the meeting, love?" I say to Enver, watching him slide his nonexistent hips easily between the front of the car and the wall I've parked too close to.

"Okay," he replies, slipping into the passenger seat and sniffing Zora's head.

"I'm so proud of him," I tell Jimmy with a smile so wide it makes my cheeks ache. He's listening but saying nothing. Seen it all, heard it all before.

"He's doing really well." I reach over and put my hand on Enver's leg, trying to ignore the shocking hardness of his femur through his ripped jeans. Solidarity. Family. Love. Recovery. I want Jimmy to see that it's all working out. I don't want him to think the things I think he thinks about me. I'm not one of those idiots, those weak women mindlessly chasing after some hapless dolt. I *love* Enver. We're a family and he's really going to do it this time. With my love and support, he'll realise there's so much to want to stay clean for. I catch sight of myself in the wing mirror. My lips are pulled so wide all my teeth are showing.

"And what about you?" Jimmy asks, dropping his cigarette butt into the drain between his feet. "You get any help yet?"

I start to mumble something about having my hands full with

Zora and being buried under piles of nappies but he shuts me down.

"Stop fucking about," he says bluntly but not unkindly. "Get to a support meeting, because if you don't, you two don't stand a chance. You're as sick as he is." He thrusts a yellow, tobacco-stained forefinger into the car towards Enver.

"I know," I say. "You're right" – even though I know nothing of the sort and want to tell Jimmy to go fuck himself.

But, as we're driving home, I begin to wonder whether he might have a point. Not about me being as sick as Enver, but about going to a support group. Perhaps it wouldn't be a bad idea. To show Enver what this has all come to, that I'm now having to take our new baby to *drug* meetings. It would also show him, of course, *my* commitment – despite everything he's done – to him and us. That I'm willing to do this for him, to support him in staying off the drugs, which might make him more inclined to stick at it. I could lead by example. Coerce by example. Control by example. Also, since so many of the family support groups are held at the same venues as *his* meetings, he wouldn't have any excuses. I really think I might be on to something, but in reality all that's happening is that, without malice or conscience and out of sheer desperation, the manipulatee is becoming the manipulator.

The following evening, we strap Zora into her car seat and drive to another meeting, this time at a school close to where Enver's mom lives. It's a group I used to attend years ago when I first got sober. Back then, there were a lot of old-timers at the meeting. People with 10, 15, 20 years of sobriety under their belts. As we pull into the car park, I pray that this is still the case and hope that some of their collective experience rubs off on Enver. Also, I say to myself, unclicking Zora's car seat and covering her with a blanket, old-timers are far more likely to see through any of his bullshit. As always, I'm so completely

185

preoccupied with life as it affects *him* that I've long been lost to myself.

His meeting takes place in a large hall on the ground floor, while the one for family and friends happens in a classroom upstairs. Leaving Enver puffing determinedly on a cigarette downstairs, I take Z up to the first floor. Inside, the meeting set-up is standard. A group of chairs in a circle and some laminated slogans of encouragement dotted about on the floor. "Let Go and Let God!", "Detach with Love", "Easy Does It".

Although I've been in hundreds, *thousands*, of these types of meetings over the years, I hover awkwardly at the door, not knowing what to do with my feet. I'm about to back out of the whole idea and go back to sitting in the car when I spot a small, slightly hunched woman with a pointy nose smiling up at me from beneath a pair of round varifocals. She looks like a bespectacled mole.

"Is this your first meeting?"

I nod.

"Take a seat – you're welcome here," she says pulling a chair out of the circle and gesturing me to sit. Z is awake, but drowsy. I crouch down, lift her out of her seat and put her to my shoulder, lowering us both into the chair.

There are still a couple of minutes before the meeting starts and so I sit, patting Z softly on her back, watching as more people arrive. They are all women. Most of them definitely don't look on the outside like I feel on the inside. They don't look like they're at breaking point. They don't look like they're living on the very brink of their lives. They're smiling, greeting, hugging – some are even laughing. Moving with ease as if they don't have the full weight of the world pressing its unforgiving knee into their backs. What the hell have they got to smile about? Clearly, whoever the addicted person is in their lives, they aren't as bad as Enver. Jimmy had promised me I'd find people here who know what I'm going through, but these women don't have a clue. Life with an addict never gives you anything to be jovial about. Maybe their addicts are doing addiction-lite.

There *are* others – two or three older women, perhaps in their late fifties or early sixties – who look tired. Dejected. But they make me even more miserable. Is this what I'm going to become, I wonder? I don't want this to be me. Sitting in rooms like this for the rest of my life. Holding out hope for the hopeless.

I feel bleak, *really* bleak, and more alone than I have the capacity to process. It's as if the life raft I've managed to pull Zora and myself onto as the ship was sinking is being dragged further out to sea towards a moody horizon. Soon, the raft too will sink and we will simply slip, helpless and hollowed, into the dark blue beneath, where the things with teeth and tentacles will claim us.

Suddenly the overhead light is switched off and someone lights the candle in the middle of the circle. A tall, striking woman with long salt-and-pepper hair asks everyone to take a seat. Even in the quieted light of the classroom I can see that her brow is unfurrowed, her whole face, in fact, relaxed, and, unlike mine, showing none of the fraught anxiety that has made a home on my forehead and ticks away in my jaw like a metronome. Her sense of peace vibrates across the circle towards me.

"Good evening, family, my name is Esther."

"Hello, Esther," choruses the room.

"My 36-year-old son and his wife are addicts in active addiction – these meetings help me detach with love."

She smiles and turns to the woman to her left who introduces herself in a similar way. Each member of the circle follows suit until it gets to me.

"I see we have a new member this evening, family," says Esther. "Is this your first meeting?" she asks me. "Would you like to introduce yourself so we can get to know you?"

Everyone turns to look at me.

"Uhm, my name is Sara ..."

I never refer to myself simply as Sara, but it's out of the question that I can reveal my full name. Sara-Jayne is just too distinctive, and I would be mortified if anyone recognised me from the radio. It's not pride, it's shame. I feel like a fraud because ever since *Killing Karoline* came out, I've bleated on about how important it is to live out loud and authentically, moving through life "in one's truth" regardless of what others might think. But not this, this is *too* authentic.

"My name is Sara and I'm ... I'm ..."

My tongue feels thick in my mouth, like a rolled-up wet sock.

Start again, maybe no one noticed.

"My name is Sara and I'm ... I'm ..."

Oh God. Get it together, SJ, this is embarrassing.

"My name is Sara and I'm ... I'm ... I'm really grateful for the meeting."

Jesus. What a cop-out. So many years of sitting in circles like this, with my ass on chairs like this, in rooms like these and I *still* don't know who the fuck I am?

"Hi, Sara," the entire room choruses back at me. "Welcome."

I *do* know who I am, though, and somewhere – in a part of my psyche that trauma is, for now, making impossible to access – I *know* why I'm here, even if I can't quite say it yet.

I pull my face into what I hope is a grateful smile and push my thumbnail between my top and bottom teeth. I'm grateful that the room is almost pitch dark save for the shrunken, lopsided candle burning in the middle of the circle. Its flame is twitching and flickering, ebbing out its last on the wooden floorboards on top of a laminated poster that reads *Keep it Simple*. I will later learn that the candle is supposed to represent the way out of the darkness and chaos of addiction and into the light of recovery. Right now, though, I have to stop myself from leaning forward in my seat, reaching for the flaming wick and squeezing the remainder of the light out of the room between my thumb and forefinger.

"Would you like to tell us why you're here, Sara?" coaxes Esther gently.

"My ... my daughter's father [I can't bring myself to call him my boyfriend, or worse, my partner] is ... he ... he's ... he's downstairs," I stutter. "In the other meeting." It's all I can manage. Esther smiles at me and nods.

"You're in the right place," says a voice across the circle. There are murmurs of agreement.

As the introductions continue around the circle, I think about what else I could have said. The things I could have, as I have before, entered into the space after my name. The -isms (to varying degrees of unmanageability) I've collected over the years: addict, alcoholic, anorexic, bulimic, compulsive overeater, over-exerciser, love addict, sex addict, sex *and* love addict, hoarder, shopaholic, gambling addict (probably, because there was that time in Vegas at the blackjack table when things nearly went to shit and I vowed never to shoot my shot in a casino ever again), workaholic, oh, and self-harmer. The full kit and kaboodle of dysfunction. But now it seems I've peaked. I've hit the motherload of fucked-up-ness because now I'm bringing my newborn baby along for the hell ride. This, here, must surely be my rock bottom?

After everyone has introduced themselves, there are a few readings. They all seem to be about learning how to "detach" in a loving way from the person with the addiction and how the only answer really is to focus on oneself.

"But don't you understand?" I want to scream. *"I can't do that! Without him, I've got no one and I can't do this alone!"*

I sit in anticipation of when these women with their smiles and misplaced levity will tell me what I need to do to stop Enver ever taking drugs again. They don't. Instead, they talk about how coming to the meetings helps them to live full, even *happy* lives regardless of what the addict is doing. Clean or sober, loaded or straight. They set themselves apart from the chaos. They have no expectations.

This is fucked up, I think, rolling my eyes back into my skull. I don't want to learn how to live with this shit; I want Enver to realise the damage he's done, get himself together and be the person I need him to be. No expectations? He's a father! I *expect* him to act like one. I'm nowhere near being able to see that I'm in a shit ton of denial that prevents me from facing the stark reality of just how far down the scale he has gone. Regardless of what I need or Enver wants or anyone expects, he *cannot* give what he does not have. And right now he does not have the capacity for anything beyond Enver.

I sit in a state of despondency until Esther tells us that the time is up. "We've come to the end of our meeting," she says. "Let's close in our usual way."

Everyone stands, reaching out their arms left and right, feeling in the dim light for the hand of the person next to them. I feel soft, slim fingers slide into my left hand and, without even being aware of doing it, grip it so tight that I feel the body it belongs to flinch but not let go. My right arm is occupied, taken hostage by a sleeping Z, but the woman next to me puts her hand on my shoulder, completing the circle.

"Let's have a moment of silence for babies conceived and born into addiction and for those still struggling with the disease of addiction," says Esther softly.

Babies conceived and born into addiction.

It's a familiar saying in groups like this and, again, one I've heard countless times before. Usually, it conjures up an image in my mind's eye of a reed-thin crack whore birthing a mewling, puce baby onto a filthy mattress in a crack den. Today, to my absolute horror, I realise it's Zora. I can't stop the tears. I am a terrible mother. The hand in mine gives it a tight squeeze.

"Let's say the Serenity Prayer," says Esther.

"God, grant me the serenity to *accept the things I cannot change, courage to change the things I can, and the wisdom to know the difference."*

Serenity, courage and wisdom. I'm lacking all three.

Someone switches the light back on and the room becomes a classroom again. I wipe my eyes, carefully place Z back into her carrier and try, as inconspicuously as possible, to make my exit.

"Keep coming back!" calls out Esther. "It works if you work it."

I meet Enver downstairs by the car.

"How was your meeting?" we both blurt out.

"It was okay," I say, glad that it's too dark for him to see my red eyes. "Yours?"

"Also okay."

"Okay."

"Yeah, okay."

And so "okay" is what we settle for.

21

Will the real Enver please stand up?

"Are you my girlfriend?"

Enver's voice filters through from the lounge. He's whispering.

"Are you? Are you my girlfriend?"

It's early. I'm lying in bed, listening.

The bedroom window is open and splinters of light are intermittently escaping from the edges of the bespoke velvet blinds I paid way too much for when I was pregnant and nesting. Every time the breeze catches the bottom of the blind, it's like an interrogation at the hands of the morning light.

"I love you, my baby."

I lie still, just listening.

"I *love* you," he says again.

I hear Zora gurgle.

"My *babatjie*. Come to Dadda," he coos. "My beautiful baby."

Another contented gurgle.

This has become their regular morning rhythm. For the last couple of weeks, the three of us have fallen into a routine of sorts, one that looks as close to normal living as we have managed to achieve for some time. Every morning, Enver, who has always been an early riser, wakes up with Zora, fishing her out of her cot at the side of our bed and taking her into the living room for a bottle so I can sleep a little longer.

During the day, we potter. A trip to the supermarket, a walk in the park, home to binge-watch a series while the baby sleeps or feeds. Once or twice we visit Sheila and I parade a newly clean Enver around like a shiny new penny.

My "muggle" friends (the nickname I give non-addicts) are delighted at this turn of events. "All he needed was to see what he would be losing," they say. "Zora will give him something to live for."

My friends in recovery are more circumspect – "It's great that he's clean, but look after *yourself* ... make *Zora* your focus, not him" – so I tend to avoid them as much as possible.

Once or twice, some of my own friends pop by to see the baby. These visits are skin-crawlingly awkward for everyone and usually result in Enver retreating to the bedroom for the duration to "pack away the laundry" or for some other spurious reason. I'm embarrassed and think he's being rude. In a moment of rare and seemingly genuine vulnerability, he tells me it's because he's filled with shame, and not just because of his heroin chic skinniness and sparse, ill-fitting wardrobe. "They must hate me for what I did," he frets. I want to tell him he ought to be more concerned with what *I* think, but instead I say, "They're not like that." But I get it. Plus, with shame being such a fueller of addiction, I decide to put an end to the friendly visitors. Just the three of us is fine. Anything to keep the peace. Anything to keep *him*.

Sometimes, I watch as Enver moves around the house like a normal person, a partner, a father, doing normal partner/father things, looking like he belongs here. Shaking out the doormat, tightening a screw on a loose cupboard door in "our" bedroom, replacing a toilet roll in the bathroom. At other times, he looks and feels like the visitor he is, on the edge, looking in on me and Z, an outsider in the home – the life – I have created for us while he was missing in action.

One day we're out in the car. As usual, Enver is driving. We pull up at the traffic lights and I see the reflection of my car in the large, tinted window of the people carrier next to us. The curve of the glass means we're a little misshapen, but I'm struck by how *ordinary* we look. Is this what other people see, I wonder, from the *outside*? The light in our lane turns green and we pull away from ourselves. The outside version of us is left behind, waiting for its own signal to go.

At home I'm still exuding an enormous amount of energy trying to manufacture the perfect climate for Enver's sobriety to stick. I try desperately to be bright and light and easy-breezy, not wanting him to have to feel any of the dark, hard heaviness that *I'm* feeling, lest it makes him disappear. So I make sure there are cigarettes on demand, coffee too. I buy him tackies and a hoody, hoping he'll feel less self-conscious about his appearance, and tell him *constantly*, sycophantically (disingenuously), what a fantastic father he is, willing it to be so and for both of us to believe it.

Never mind what the support groups keep trying to tell me, I think, this – the "okay-making" of everything for Enver – *this* will be what keeps our little family together. This will be the thing that makes him see, and *stay*. If he really loves us, he will see how hard I'm trying to make this work, in spite of everything. Is it ideal? No. Is it exhausting and a complete betrayal of myself and my truth? Yes. Am I able to do things any other way right now? Not a fuck.

In the evenings, Enver cooks supper while I feed and bathe Zora, and then we all get in the car and go to our upstairs-downstairs meetings. We do it most nights and it's even gotten to the point where I've begun to look forward to sitting in the candle circle, seeing the same friendly, now-familiar faces night after night. In addition to the fact that everyone in the meeting makes a huge fuss of Z and jostle good-heartedly for an opportunity to hold

194

her, their hugs and kind smiles and maternal warmth fill the mother-shaped gap in my life that is adding to my feelings of desolation.

The meetings offer me a break from the constant closeness of Enver, which I need but which also suffocates me. They also become a safe space where I can breathe and cry and grieve and rant and, once in a while, even laugh like the others do. In some small way, the groups are helping. The sharing of stories lets me know that other people's days are filled with some of the same struggles, but I'm still unable to believe there's nothing definitive *I* can do to make sure Enver stays straight for good. You're powerless over him and his using, I'm told. No, I think, I just haven't found the Achilles heel of his addiction. Yet.

For the most part, we are putting on a fairly convincing performance of *Happy Families*. The sheer relief of not having to be a first-time mother on my own (plus the brain-altering impact of the horror of the past few months) means I simply try to grin and bear the other stuff. Occasionally, however, we fall out of character and the masks slip. Behind the scenes, things can erupt. Fast. A skew look, an off-key comment from Enver, and a rage and hatred so fierce that I'm unable to contain it comes boiling fervidly to the surface. A volcano of loathing.

Every morning I wake up and tell myself not to lose it, not to react, believing that if I do, I risk pushing him towards the drugs. But then he says or does something or maybe even nothing at all (sometimes it's just his presence that triggers me) and it's like he's pouring caustic acid on an open sore. A switch flips in my brain.

"I despise you!" I seethe.

"I hope you die and your mother has to identify your body in a morgue."

When he doesn't flinch, I dig deeper, reaching down into the shit-filled sewer of my damaged psyche and pulling out the most putrid filth. Stuff that, when I hurl it, will stick to him and leave the stench of my festering wounds all over his new hoody.

"There's a special place in hell for people like you and your godawful family – I hope you all die and I will dance on your graves."

My venomous vitriol is made all the more impactful due to the fact I'm whispering it through clenched teeth so that I will not alert Zora to the complete dysfunction of her despicable parents.

"No wonder you turned out the way you did, no fucking surprises there!"

"You *disgust* me! Why don't you just kill yourself, you worthless, deceitful, useless *cunt*!"

It's everything I'd felt and wanted to say to him during the very worst times of my pregnancy. I vomit it all out like morning sickness.

But even while I'm raging, I'm always terrified of pushing him over the edge. It's the most fucked-up game I play with myself. Push and push and push to see what will be the thing that tips him over the edge, while simultaneously I'm terrified of saying the very thing that will make him disappear. Between the uncontrollable rage and the anxiety of being left again, it becomes a constant battle between two different states of desperation.

And then there are the moments, like now, listening to him chatting to Zora, just the two of them in the magical space before the world has woken up, bringing with it its noise and fog, that I'm reminded of the Enver from "before". The Enver I fell tender-heart and crazy-head for. The one who promised me bubble baths and head kisses, strong arms and home, and I wonder whether it can possibly be that same man, *this* man with the gentle voice and adoring words, who has wreaked so much havoc on us.

These moments leave me so confused. *How* is this the same person who did all those terrible things? This man who cradles our baby in the crook of his arm as if it were created for that purpose alone, who calms her when she cries and who so gently manoeuvres her floppy little body into her sleep suit at night before kissing her softly on her downy head. Is it the same person? Who, in fact, is the real Enver?

Is it this guy, the one sitting in my living room rocking our daughter on his skeletal chest and, if so, how can I be sure? And, if it *is* really him, then how do I destroy the deceitful, violent imposter who seems determined to take him hostage, without killing them both?

"Daddy's baby, *ek is lief vir jou.*"

With my ear pressed up against the walls of this tender father-daughter moment, I ask myself whether this is who Enver is when no one's looking. When the weight (imagined or otherwise) of judgment, expectation, disappointment and hope is lifted. Is this the Enver it requires the least energy to be? I'm shattered. It hurts my heart to see the effort it takes for him to live every day as the version of himself he believes is acceptable. The unrelenting labour of living a lie.

On the day of Zora's four-week check-up at the paediatrician, Enver is also due to have a medical exam. It's a requirement of one of the treatment facilities to which he's applied. His appointment is at the government health clinic close to the private hospital where Zora's doctor has her rooms. He suggests he heads through early to make sure he's one of the first in line. "The queues will be murder," he tells me. "I'll go now and be back in time for us to go to the appointment with Zora at midday."

It sounds like a plan. I'm so proud that he's actually doing this. One step closer to rehab, one step closer to rescuing me from single motherhood and one step closer to making sure I never have to tell Zora that Daddy is an emaciated smack fiend, or worse, that he *was* when he was alive.

Enver inhales two cups of hot coffee and heads for the clinic. I wave him off and remind him he needs to be back by 11:30am at the latest or we'll be late.

"I'll be here, I promise."

I spend the first couple of hours in "doing" mode. While Z sleeps, I wash and fold one hundred babygros and scrub every single one of her bottles with sterilising solution until my fingers are wrinkled and my hands covered in a film of white. Then I repack her cupboards, rearranging the million bottles of baby bubble bath I was given at my baby shower.

At 10:30am, I put Z in the bassinet on the bathroom floor while I shower.

At 11am, I put her on the bed while I get dressed and dry my hair.

At 11:15am, I take four chicken breasts out of the freezer to defrost for supper.

At 11:20am, I reply to an SMS from the guy who cuts my lawn: *Thursday 2pm.* 👍

At 11:25am, I pack the car with Zora's baby bag and slip her medical book into my handbag.

At 11:30am, I put Zora in the car.

At 11:40am, I take Zora out of the car.

At 11:45am, I walk to the gate and look left and right down the road, just to check.

At 11:50am, I put Zora back in the car and drive to our appointment.

When we finally arrive at the hospital 20 minutes late, the doctor asks how things are going.

"Fine," I say. "Her dad couldn't make it today because of work," I offer by way of an explanation no one asked for.

I watch as every inch of Zora's tiny body is meticulously examined. She's weighed and measured, toe to crown. Only when the doctor finally pulls the stethoscope out of her ears and folds it into her lap do I realise I've been holding my breath.

"Well," she says, "she's absolutely perfect. Well done, Mom, good job."

I burst into tears and we leave.

At 2pm, I tell myself he's probably still waiting to be seen by a doctor.

At 3pm, I'm cursing myself for being too pig-headed to buy him (another) cell phone.

At 4pm, I'm Googling *closing times for government clinics*.

At 5pm, I realise this is the longest Zora and I have ever been on our own together.

At 6pm, I cook two of the four chicken breasts and eat half of one.

At 7pm, I realise he's not coming back.

And at 7:45pm, because I don't know what else to do, I say the Serenity Prayer, buckle Zora into the car seat and drive to a meeting.

22

It'll be lonely this Christmas

"Come home," I say. I cannot stop the words sneaking out of my treacherous mouth.

Home, SJ? You cannot be serious?

It's taken eight days. Eight days for him to get in touch. Eight days since he left us to head back out there, to *it*.

Eight days since he jumped out of the driving seat of the bumper car while it was still moving to go and get high on the Ferris wheel, up-up-up and away. Away from us, away from himself and into the rain clouds. Eight days and now, despite the warning signs telling me "this ride is broken", I'm about to get back on. His disease compels him to always run away; mine compels me to always chase him.

"We miss you."

Who is "we"? Because it's not you, SJ, not the real you, not the one you keep abandoning for this hell show and, at barely four weeks old, it can't really be Zora, can it? She only exists for your welcoming, milk-ripe breasts, not for her drug-addled, heroin-whipped, chaos-bringing father.

"Can you fetch me from my mom in an hour?" says Enver.

That's only seven minutes away. Why does he need a whole hour? You know why, SJ.

"Sure," I reply, fake casual, already scanning the lounge for my car keys. The th-thump, th-thump, th-thump that I have come to convince myself is excitement and longing but which is really anxiety and trepidation, begins its familiar beat under my collarbone.

"Okay, see you in an hour then," he replies.

Zora gurgles hiccups in the corner, reminding me, finally, that I have a daughter. I smile at her.

"Cool." I exhale, relieved at having staved off another evening of single parenthood, click off the call and do my best to close my ears to the internal, interminable, too honest voice in my head.

None of this is cool, SJ, you fucking lunatic.

I clock-watch for 53 minutes and then bundle Zora into the car, telling her "We're going to see Daddy" in a singsong voice. She blinks at me and yawns.

When I was a child, I was endlessly fascinated by the macabre. Real dark stuff. Serial killers especially. They captivated me. The more heinous and gruesome their crimes, the better. I wanted to know exactly how this one had removed his victim's eyeballs with a Swiss Army knife, or how that one had had sex with the decomposing skull of the family dachshund. The horror of their wicked acts both fascinated and disgusted me. Other people's twisted psyches and depravity. How could they *do* the things they did and still sleep at night? It was the stuff of nightmares, frequently mine, and I would have a hard time leaving the headless, eyeless, fingerless victims of these crazies in the pages of the books and magazines where I found them. More often than not, I would end up taking them to bed with me, where they would elbow their way into my dreams, forcing me to become an unwilling spectator, and sometimes, worse, even an accomplice to a catalogue of unimaginable evils. But despite the inevitable nightmares, I'd always go back, would always want to see more, more guts and innards, more suffering. I was simply unable to resist the urge to traumatise myself.

I was also a nosy child. "Inquisitive", I imagine it would have said on my school report: "*Sara-Jayne is a curious, inquisitive child.*" It was this curiosity that would have me poring over the reports Mum would bring home with her after a day at work, social-working and fixing the unmanageable lives of the great unwashed. Worked to the bone on a civil-servant salary, she'd frequently be forced to finish these reports at our dining-room table, often long into the night.

Sometimes she'd leave them open while she cooked dinner and I would strategically place myself in her vacant seat, on the premise of doing homework while, in fact, speed-reading the details of some fucked-up family's dysfunction as seen through the eyes of my mother. Save for names and places, most of the reports seemed to follow the same tragic storyline: young girl gets knocked up by hopeless, hapless criminal/drug addict/paedophile and ends up in a relentless cycle of abuse and misery, unable to summon the intestinal fortitude to do the right thing and leave the useless dolt. My teenage judgment was always the same. What sort of pathetic, selfish, fucked-up excuse for a mother chooses a man over her own children? Scum. Of. The. Earth. That's who, I reasoned. There was never any consideration of why these women might be "choosing" these men at the expense of themselves or their kids, just disgust at their weakness.

I make a right turn into the road where Enver's mother lives, almost tapping my feet in time to the thumping in my chest. I foresee what's about to happen and tell myself it's perception rather than history that's allowing me such foresight, as if that somehow absolves me of the responsibility for what I'm doing. I already know he's not there, and I know why.

Car still running, I wait outside the house for five minutes. It's out of the question that I will go and knock on the door. The hatred and rage I still feel towards his mother prickles the skin of my neck. Zora is more than a month old and there's been absolutely no word from *any* of his family. No congratulations, no inquiry, nothing. I don't even know if they know her name.

I honk the horn, jolting awake a sleeping Zora. I can't bear to sit in the silence too long; I know what will happen, and it does.

What sort of pathetic, selfish ...

HONNNNKKKK!

... fucked-up excuse for a mother ...

HONK-HONNNKKK!

... chooses a man over her own children?

HONK-HONK-HOONNNNKKK!

Scum. Of. The. Earth.

Three agonising minutes later, Enver appears in the rearview mirror, heading up the road behind us. He's in the car before I can catch my breath.

"I was just getting cigarettes," he lies.

Cool.

I instantly notice he's back to his "street" uniform of tatty flip-flops, faded T-shirt and too-short track pants. The trainers and hoody I'd bought him a few weeks back have clearly been sacrificed to the temple of skag.

I rev the engine and pull away, punching "CD" on the entertainment system. Whitney Houston springs into action, posthumously filling the car with a soaring vibrato, but she's not loud enough.

You're as bad as him. In fact, you're worse. He may always be running away, but you're the one running after him – into the fire, with your baby strapped to your back.

Exactly seven weeks after Z is born, we are preparing to spend our first Christmas together as a family. I've allowed denial, sentimentality and the festive spirit to get the better of me and have forgotten that rarely do good tidings, Yuletide cheer and heroin addiction come without strings attached and the prospect of tensions running high. Even for normal families – which I am under no illusion we are – Christmas can be fraught with expectation, overcooked turkey and disappointment.

Burying my anxiety under excessive amounts of tinsel and Hallmark-card festive merriment, I get up early to peel potatoes and wrap Enver's gift. It's a picture, a photograph of him and Zora taken late one evening when we first brought her home from the hospital, in that strange period when day was indistinguishable from night.

I'd had plenty of images to choose from. My phone is filled with photos of them both. She's not even two months old, but there are literally thousands. Capturing the two of them together, immortalising them, has become an obsession. I'm terrified that if I don't, it might never have happened.

I've had the photo printed in black and white (for maximum effect) and put it in a frame along with a note on the back, ostensibly from Zora, which reads, "No one will ever love you the way I do, Daddy." It's a desperate move, but I am desperate. I really believe it might work. Everything is a manipulation now. Him of me, me of him. Us of ourselves.

I wrap the frame, the picture and the note – careful to avoid rustling too loudly a hundred goofy-looking skiing Rudolphs – and place it strategically on the bookshelf, just above the enormous, pointless felt stocking I've bought for Zora. I pop on a Santa hat, for levity, pick up a knife and start slicing.

I have a weird relationship with Christmas. I love and dread it in equal measure. When I was 11, my dad, Malcolm, decided that the post-lunch gift-opening lull on Christmas Day – when we were all stuffed with moderately undercooked turkey and still gleaming with festive cheer – would be the ideal time to announce to my brother and me that he and my mother were getting a divorce. After passing an almighty shit in the upstairs bathroom, he padded into the dining room in his regulation moccasins, tissue-paper crown balanced precariously on his head, a globule of my grandmother's potent brandy butter in his beard, and declared, "There's going to be a divorce." At opposite ends of the dining table, my brother and I sat and blinked at one another. After that, for many, many years, Christmas just became another 24 hours to endure. Fah-la-la-la-la-la-la-la-la.

I'm humming Christmas carols when Enver walks in carrying Z. I stop peeling and turn around. I don't really need to – I feel him before I see him these days. He's a presence rather than a person. It's almost as if he's haunting me while his heart still beats behind his ribs. The living dead.

Z is wearing a mini Santa hat and a babygro that says "My first Christmas". Holding her against his chest with one hand, he clicks the TV on with the other. *Home Alone.*

"I'm going to visit my mommy and them," Enver announces a little after 2pm.

Until five minutes ago we'd been lying on the sofa after a generous lunch, my feet in his lap, Z fast asleep in her bassinet on the floor. He sits up, running his hands through his hair. I wish he'd cut it, and his beard; he looks wild.

"I'm gonna go," he says again. "I'll be back later."

Deck the halls with boughs of holly, fah-la-la-la-la-la-la-la-la.

"Why don't I drop you there?" I suggest.

'Tis the season to be jolly, fah-la-la-la-la-la-la-la-la.

"It's okay, I'll walk."

"Why don't you go tomorrow?"

Don we now our gay apparel, fah-la-la-la-la-la-la-la-la.

"It's my family. I'm allowed to see my family on Christmas Day," he snaps, sliding on his flip-flops.

Fah-la-la-la-la-la-la-la-la. Fuck.

"Please don't do this." I know better than to read from this script, but I can't stop myself.

"I'm not doing anything. I'm just going to visit my mom." His eyes have gone black.

8, 9, 10 … 11, 12, 1, 2. Six hours. He's managed a little over six hours.

I'm running out of straws to clutch.

"It's Zora's first Christmas – please, *please* don't."

"*Stop it!*" he bellows. I flinch and then start crying fat, redundant tears. I know this is only going to end one way.

I don't even see him leave, but I can feel he's gone.

Zora stirs in her bassinet, moving her little fists towards her mouth. I lift her out and settle back down on the sofa while she feeds.

I press "Standby" on the TV remote and the screen blinks awake. *Home Alone* again. It's on repeat.

A few days later, we usher in the New Year, just the two of us, me and Z. We haven't seen or heard from Enver since he walked out on Christmas Day. In fact, we haven't spoken to or seen another person for the past six days. Just going through the motions. On the morning of the 31st, an old friend from rehab, whom I haven't seen in years, invites us to spend the night with her and her two kids at her place on the other side of Cape Town. I say yes immediately. When we get there, she's pissed as a fart and clearly ready for a night of jolling, not sober, single-mother solidarity, so I make an excuse and bundle Z back into the car and drive home.

Neither of us actually makes it to midnight, which is a relief. I don't think I can bear the official ring-a-ding-ding chiming in of both a new year and my abject loneliness. Before I fall asleep, finally putting to bed 12 agonising months I wasn't sure I would survive, I wonder whether there is any credence to something I remember hearing once that, whoever you are with as the clock strikes midnight on New Year's Eve is the person with whom you will spend the coming year. I can't help but wonder whether the opposite is true. Does the fact that I am alone, without Enver, mean we'll spend the next 12 months without him too? Will 12 months turn into 12 years, 12 years a slave to wondering why we weren't enough? Too tired for more tears, I shut the door on the prospect, roll over and drift into dreamless, hauntingly empty sleep, Z breathing deeply but contentedly in her bassinet next to my bed.

23

Just the lonely talking again

If I had thought pregnancy was lonely, single-handedly parenting a newborn takes things to a whole other level. First, there's the absolute vulnerability, dependence and soft-skulledness of Zora, which makes me physically tremble. All the time she'd been inside my body, even as I grew bigger, I could pretend she wasn't really there. I knew she was safe, so I was able to check out when the sharpness of my desperation felt as if it would slice me into pieces.

While she was a passenger, I was free to wallow, or howl or dissociate to my broken heart's content. Days in a row I could switch off for hours on end, either doggedly burying myself in work or zoning out in front of mindless nonsense on Netflix or how-to videos on YouTube. How To: Draw the perfect eyebrow. How To: Remove the stone from an avocado without a knife. How To: Survive the devastation of the love of your life abandoning you during pregnancy to a fevered and unforgiving heroin addiction. But now that she's here, things are different. Every second has her in it. Innocent, needy, terrifying. The all-and-everythingness of it takes my breath away.

Before I was pregnant, I often heard people speak of the absolute, overwhelming love one experiences for a child the second it is either pushed or pulled from you and that, once you set eyes on them, there is no other love like it in the world. It's true, of course, but it's not the full story. What most people fail to tell you about – perhaps because it's almost impossible to accurately put into words – is, more than the love, the unrelenting, kick-you-in-the-ass, gun-to-your-head type fear delivered along with the child.

I first felt it four days after bringing Zora home from the hospital. We were both still fairly woozy from the anaesthetic and the pain pills they'd thrust into my hands and instructed me to take three times a day (and which, miraculously, Enver hadn't inhaled as soon as my aching back was turned). Zora was asleep in her bassinet on the living-room floor, and I was in my bedroom smearing cream on my raw, ravaged nipples. I tiptoed back in to check on her, smiling as I peered into her blanketed cocoon on the floor, but when I looked down, she wasn't moving. Not a flicker of her long lashes across her cheeks, nor even the slightest rise and fall of her chest under the hospital blanket I'd inadvertently taken with me when we were discharged. Just stillness. And then a sensation that felt as though someone had drawn a knife down between my shoulder blades and drained the lifeblood from me. She's dead, was my immediate thought. In a nanosecond, I envisaged myself standing alone beside a tiny coffin, then packing away into boxes all the baby-related *accoutrements* I'd spent the last nine months accumulating, writing a short but self-explanatory suicide note and blowing my brains out with a gun I'd acquired for cash from a tall Angolan down a side street off Wynberg Main Road. All of it in that minute fragment of our enormous lives.

"Zora!" I bellowed, dropping down and shoving her tiny shoulders, hard. She barely even stirred, just reorganised her fragile fingers into a looser fist and shifted slightly under the stolen blanket. The relief of it, of life, took my feet out from under me and I sobbed for a good 10 minutes on the rug next to her, completely winded and utterly horrified by my first true glimpse at what my life now looked like through the filter of parenthood. Zora was fine, but I was forever changed. That feeling, that *fear*, was such that for a moment I ceased even to exist.

Prior to having her, I often thought and suspected that if ever I were to become a parent, I was likely to be the fearful, neurotic kind (very unlike my own parents whose *laissez-faire* parenting I've felt both affronted by and grateful for at various points in my life). I rationalised that the effect of losing the most important person in my life before I could even speak was likely to rear its head with a vengeance if ever I had my own child. I would sometimes imagine waving my hypothetical kid off to school and then sitting for seven hours in anxious anticipation of their return, biting my nails to the quick, terrified they would fall victim to some or other misfortune or mischief. School trips would be out of the question, naturally. So too sleepovers and any activity involving anything fast-moving or taking place above waist height. Pretty much all normal childhood activities, anything that would contribute to my imaginary child developing a healthy sense of adventure and blossoming into a well-rounded individual, would be out of the question thanks to my neurosis. These daydreams featuring my future parenting self (and the lifelong fear I held that the ability to abandon one's child might be genetic) usually ended with the realisation and resignation that it would be better if I never had my own children.

Although the entire bassinet incident was over in the time it had taken me to take a single breath, it marked a turning point for me. There was now a time before the fear and a time after it, *the rest of my life*, and it was all compounded by the fact that the only other person in the world who was supposed to feel it with the same keenness *I* had in that moment had left me completely alone while he smoked his own fears away on the same foil I'd used to cook the Christmas turkey.

The other type of loneliness I felt caught me far less unawares. It was the loneliness I'd anticipated and feared for years – from the first time I'd peed into a pot all those years ago and seen the oh-shit-fuck-shit possibility of single teen parenthood looming on the horizon, up until the second I'd found out the truth about Enver and his drug use.

Despite everyone's assurances during my pregnancy that the arrival of Zora would be the magic wand that would swish-swish-flick away all the bad and dread anticipation of doing it alone, it is as desperate as I'd imagined. It has nothing to do with Zora and me or our developing mother-daughter bond. That appears to be progressing as it should. Although, as anyone who's had a baby will attest, those early days of the "fourth trimester" are largely a groundhog day of feeding and arse wiping and a distinct lack of reciprocity as far as smiles and goo-goo-gaa-gaa baby talk go.

Nor is it that Zora is a "difficult" baby. She isn't. Actually, she's a dream. Sleeping well, practically burping on command, and delivering the required number of pee and poo-filled nappies every day. In fact, she's *so* agreeable that I often wonder whether the universe, understanding how precariously on the edge of unravelling I am, has conspired to cut me some slack with an "easy" baby. "Super chilled" is how several friends describe her when they pop in to see us. As a first-time mom and not being someone who's spent a lot of time around babies, I have no frame of reference and so, among the fucked-uppedness of everything, I frequently thank heavens for Zora's chill factor.

But her easy-going nature doesn't eliminate the abject terror or breathtaking grief I feel enveloped by when it's just the two of us. Sometimes, in the middle of the night, with Zora sleeping an arm's length away, oblivious to our separation and curled up as if still in the womb, I drag the duvet over my head, pull my knees up towards my ribs and wail, my hands cupped tightly over my mouth. At other times, while she feeds, I am taunted by the stillness and barren silence of night and I slump against the pillows, counting my in breaths and wondering how many more I have until my last one. It's like *déjà vu*. These are exactly the scenes I had in mind when Enver first disappeared. This is what I had feared above anything.

I'm crippled with guilt and shame that I'm allowing my loneliness and grief to interfere with the joy of Zora being in the world. Moments that should be filled with laughter and levity, celebrating a gassy smile or a hiccup giggle, are, for me, often just seconds through which I have to survive, and I hate myself – and, of course, Enver – for that.

There's also the shame I can't ever speak of, to anyone. I'm *scared* of Zora. I love her, but I'm scared to be alone with her. I feel so lacking in what I think is required to be a mother that in the moments when it's just the two of us, I feel completely exposed. Like a spotlight is being shone on my maternal incompetence. I'm terrified that I'll do something that will show her and the rest of the world that I just don't have what it takes. At any moment I expect her to look me dead in the eye and say, "You're fucking this up. You're fucking *me* up."

A few things save me during those early, heartbreaking months when the days seem like they'll never end. Going to the gym becomes a crucial part of my survival routine. Not because I give a shit about losing "baby weight" or anything as inconsequential as fitting back into my pre-pregnancy jeans, but because, addict that I am, it's an hour a day that allows me to escape reality. It's also 60 minutes in which my body is my own again and not just the feeding station for Zora's hungry little body. Every day I drop her at the gym crèche, then head for the treadmill or the free weights where I put my headphones on and blast an angry playlist into my eardrums. I run and squat and lunge and lift until my muscles burn. Then, when I've purged and punished myself enough, I sit in the sauna, throwing ladle upon ladle of water onto the red-hot coals, sweating and revelling in the toxins leaving my body. Within two months I weigh 20 kilograms less than I had a year prior to giving birth.

The other thing that saves me is my antenatal group. While I'd been in England, a mom friend of mine had suggested I join one. "It'll be full of complete wankers," she warned, "but at least you'll know how to puff and pant when the time comes." I'd taken her advice and found a class that was being run close to my new house. For the first couple of sessions, I convinced a friend to come along with me, because I couldn't face being the only single pregnant person among a bunch of happily coupled, irritatingly enthusiastic, can't-wait-to-find-out-how-to-check-my-own/my-wife's-cervix-to-see-how-far-dilated-I-am/we-are parents-to-be. As my friend had predicted, I'd hated everyone on sight. But I'd stuck with it, and by the time the classes were over, one of the moms-to-be had added us all to a WhatsApp group so we could stay in touch and check in with each other after the babies were born. The group becomes my absolute lifeline and I know I wouldn't have survived without it.

My support meetings also help keep my head above water. Every evening after gym and having cooked myself a one-handed supper, I put Zora into her warmest onesie and we drive across Cape Town to sit with other people who know what it's like to have your life ripped apart by addiction.

As desperate as those first few months are, there *are* times when the clouds part and promises of light are able to slither through. Zora's first smile, her obvious delight when, in the morning, I beam into her cot and sing "Wakey-wakey, Zora" and she wriggles excitedly. I practically high-five a complete stranger the first time I manage to manoeuvre Zora from the car seat into the baby sling without incident. There is something so empowering about being able to overcome even the smallest of daily challenges without falling to pieces. I know that there is nothing special about me and that mothers have been doing (and doing alone) all of this since the beginning of time, but still, for me, they are victories and I claim them whenever they come. I also come to the strangely comforting realisation that no matter how much I hate myself, I'll always love Zora more.

The cliché is that you can be surrounded by people and still feel completely alone. While I am definitely not surrounded by others (I still haven't heard anything from Enver's family and have only occasional terse and perfunctory communication with my own mother), I am not completely alone either. I have my new friends from the antenatal group and, just as had happened during my pregnancy, there are a few other angels in human form who float in as light through the cracks. Most of the time, when people visit, I try to look happy and say all the right things about how fast Zora is growing and how lucky I am to have such a good sleeper. I slip quickly back into my Best Actress routine, desperate to shore up the landslide of sorrow that I know is lurking just behind the façade.

Where possible, I avoid all mention of Enver and, for the sake of decency, most of our visitors do too. Those who are able to see behind my eyes tentatively ask and, because I can't risk falling apart, I say, "I'm fine." When people say I'm doing such a great job or that Zora is lucky to have me as a mother, I don't hear them, because the fact is that there is only person in the world I want to hear say those words and he is maintaining his usual post-relapse radio silence.

One Saturday night, a couple of months into the new year, Zora is sleeping soundly, and I'm debating whether to join her or sift through my emails. I'm absolutely dreading heading back to work, but think it would be wise to get a head start on clearing the emails I'm sure have been piling up since I went on maternity leave four short months ago. I'm in two minds about what to do. It's been a really long day and I should probably just go to sleep, because tomorrow will be Groundhog Day. I've found that weekends are the worst; they tend to drag on and on, and I struggle to find ways to fill the emptiness. Sometimes, I'll end up doing two sessions at the gym, or I'll push Zora in her pram and wander aimlessly through the mall. Most of the time we end up taking a drive to the beach, where I put her in the sling and we just walk for hours until the sun tells us it's time to head home.

There's been no word from Enver since Christmas, and the anger and accompanying madness that had me by the jugular during pregnancy have begun to snake their fingers back around my neck, except this time it's worse because *this* time Enver *knows* what he's missing out on. He knows how hard this is. He knows how scared I am. He knows what the stakes are. He knows Zora.

"How can he just walk out on his own daughter?" I demand one night at my support meeting while Zora snoozes contentedly in the arms of one of the long-timers. "Doesn't he *love* her?" I've long since factored myself out of the love equation.

"Addiction is a disease," someone reminds me gently. "When our addicts behave in the most uncaring and unimaginable ways, it becomes almost impossible not to see it as personal, but we have found, actually, that addiction doesn't mean a lack of affection for the family. It's not even about love, it's about illness. They've lost the power of choice." I desperately want to believe them, and part of me does. Enver's no demon – it's *addiction* that's the devil. It's what turned my lovely, gentle big brother into a marauding terrorist in our home and it's what's robbing Zora of her daddy and me of the man who once upon a time made me smile wider and laugh louder and feel safer than anyone else on earth.

As I'm strapping Zora into the car after the meeting, I feel a hand on my back, and someone leans in close. "Don't hate the addict, hate the disease," says a voice in the dark. They mean well, of course, but it's easier said than done. So too is the concept of detaching with love, which apparently I should also be doing, but I *can't* do that so instead I continue to allow myself to be dragged along on the coat-tails of hopelessness.

The emails won't sort themselves, I decide, so I start working my way through hundreds of unopened messages. Work stuff, book stuff, I've shut off from all of it since Zora was born. There are a hundred emails from a flower company I used five years ago to send a birthday bouquet to Enver's mother and from which I've been trying to unsubscribe ever since. I'm about to mass-delete the whole lot when I notice one from a dating app that has managed to avoid the peril of my junk folder.

Maybe *this* is what I need. Maybe *this* is how I'll finally be able to detach from Enver and this misery-go-round of chaos. I've been living in denial for too long, and it's time to face the hard truth that Enver's *never* going to come right. Maybe it's time to move on. What's the saying? The best way to get over a man is to get under another? I have no desire or intention to get *under* anyone, but something needs to happen; there has to be a shift and maybe this is it.

Before I'm even aware of what I'm doing, I download the app, ignoring all the requests to fill out information about myself for potential matches. I don't care about any of that. I have to upload a picture, though. Fuck. The last time I'd looked at myself properly in the mirror, I'd been horrified. I looked every single one of my 39 years. From the two deep and distinct grooves that run like parched riverbeds in parallel across my brow to the skin above my eyes that has started to crepe and the unwanted flesh that has begun creating creases in my neck and under my chin. The jutting hip bones and washboard stomach of my anorexic twenties replaced by fat rolls and stretch marks, my whole mid-section like someone has overfilled a rubber tyre with jelly. My breasts, which have been sucked and suckled, weigh large and heavy on my front and my once firm, taut thighs meet not at the top, but just above my wrinkled knees and rub together when I walk, chafing me to hell and back.

I scroll through my phone and upload a picture from (another) solo trip I took to Mozambique three years ago. I looked tanned and happy and the right side of 35.

I mindlessly swipe left and right a few times until an animated heart beats across my screen. *You've met your match!* Then, almost instantly, a notification: *Devon wants to send you a message.* Okay, I shrug. A message pings onto my screen. I tap it. Nice-looking guy. Same age as me. I feel absolutely nothing. We exchange some small talk for a couple of minutes and then he asks me what I'm doing. I tell him I'm watching my baby sleep and clearing out my email inbox.

Devon1980CPT: Baby?

SJ: Yes.

Devon1980CPT: How old is it?

SJ: *She* is four months.

"You're disgusting," he writes. "You should be focusing on your baby, not trying to hook up with people on Tinder. You should be ashamed of yourself."

And I am. I am ashamed. Not because I'm trying to hook up with anyone (because I'm not), but because *this* is what it has come to. I immediately delete the app and lie back on the pillow, staring at the monsters projected onto the ceiling by the bedside lamp.

It's time, I realise. Time to accept that no one's coming to rescue me.

24

Locked down, fucked up

It's T-minus 21 hours from the whole country being put into lockdown and I'm praying to a God I can't bring myself to believe in to spare me from this modern-day plague of locusts. I'm four months post-partum, still feeling ripped from cunt to craw, staving off a depressive episode by the skin of my teeth and about to single-parent my way through a global pandemic.

While I've been preparing to return to work after four months' maternity leave, my colleagues in the media have been reporting on a developing news story I've only caught snippets of on the TV at the gym. Since giving birth, I've barely read a newspaper, clicked a news alert in my email inbox or intentionally listened to a news bulletin, mainly because I've been too focused on the catastrophic events making headlines in my own world.

But also, outside the chaos of Enver, having Zora has pulled my focus more inward than ever before. The major events of my day are mostly happening in or on my own body, and the two of us are literally the centre of our own universe. Life exists only in the room we're occupying at any given time. If it doesn't happen within our bubble, it may as well not have happened. But now our bubble has been burst by the arrival of something strange, unpredictable and terrifying.

I am terrified. Not of the virus, although I'm pretty fucking worried about that too, but of lockdown. All my life rafts are about to be sunk simultaneously overnight. There is to be no more gym, no more hanging out with my antenatal friends and their babies, no more support meetings. Lockdown is about to do a number on me.

The only port in the storm is the recent addition to our lives of Mavis, the woman I've hired to help me look after Zora while I do the dance-of-a-thousand jobs to keep a roof over our heads. It's a blessed relief that she loves Zora, has a cracking sense of humour and knows her way around a kitchen, but it's a few days into lockdown when I really thank God (the same nonexistent one from a couple of days ago) for her being around. It's in the evenings, with Zora swaddled and cocooned in her bassinet next to my bed, that I am the most grateful for Mavis. Knowing that on the other side of the wall that separates my white-knuckled survival from her muffled isiXhosa soapies is another adult body, a woman-mother, who knows for herself the sheer effort of my existence, gives me desperately needed comfort. But still not enough for me not to wonder, night after night, my face pressed hard into the pillow on what was, for a few fleeting nights, his side of the bed, where Enver is and if he's thinking about us at all.

One day, a few weeks into lockdown, I'm working on my bed-turned-chair on my pillow-turned-desk in my bedroom-turned-office when my phone rings. A name flashes on the screen. It's Enver's mother. I brace myself. This is it. It's finally happened. He's overdosed. Found dead in a petrol-station toilet or slumped behind the industrial waste bins at the train station. Maybe it happened weeks ago, maybe his family have already held the funeral and only decided to tell me today.

Every day I wait for that call. Sometimes I picture him laid out on a mortuary slab under a flickering, sterile blue light. He's covered with a government-issue sheet, his tar-black blood pissing out of his jugular into a drain on the grubby tiled floor. I'm peering through a window nodding, while a cop stands next to me and says something into a radio mic on his lapel. It's a scene straight out of a TV drama.

At other times, I wonder where Zora and I would sit at his funeral. Right at the back like late arrivals at the theatre, or at the front like the defendants in a murder trial? Often, I wonder whether we'd even be invited. I think about us turning up at his wake only to be shooed away, and then driving home in black and heels. An entire chicken pasta salad gone to waste, sweating on the back seat.

Poor Zora, I think, tapping the flashing green phone icon. I don't say hello; this is not news I will ever invite in by way of courteous greeting. Instead, I wait for whoever is on the other end to say the thing that will pull us into the next stage of our lives.

"Hello."

Enver.

The relief that he's not dead and that today is not the day and date that will be forever etched into our psychological calendars is immediately replaced with contempt and rage.

"Where the *fuck* have you been?" I seethe.

I jump off the bed and scoot quickly past Mavis and a giggling Zora and into the garden where I can lay into him without restraint.

"I'm sorry, love, I've been trying to come right. I didn't want to get in touch until I had. How are you? How's Zora? Are you staying safe?"

It's too much. Too many words. Too fast. I can't make sense of it all. Can't get any purchase on any one thing he's saying because the water is rising too fast, and I know I need to take one big breath and hold it so that when the water pushes over my head I'm ready for it, but I can't because my legs are kicking frantically under me to make sure that I stay afloat, but what's this ... now they feel like they're caught in something that's pulling me down and the more I kick, the harder the thing pulls. I'm going under.

"Don't you even care about your daughter, Enver?" I start to cry.

"I *do*," he implores, "but it's the drugs, love ... They turn me into a monster, but that's not who I am. I'm so sorry, baby! I'm so fucking sorry. That's not who I am."

"I don't know *who* you are, Enver."

"You *do*, baby!" he cries. "You do *know* the real me."

Do I? It's the question I've pondered over all others for the last 13 years. I *think* I do, but then ...

"I've missed you guys so much. Is Zora okay?"

"She's perfect."

"I've been speaking to Jerome ... He's helping me." I know Jerome. He's from the NA meetings – this is a good sign. "I guess you know about the online meetings since lockdown. I've being doing a few here at my mom's, but she doesn't always have data."

I have data. Better, I have Wi-Fi.

"I'm *really* gonna do it this time, love. No more fucking about. I know there's too much to lose. I love you guys. I do, baby, I love you."

"I love *you*," I say, not because I have any confidence in it being true, but because I think it's what he needs to hear and what will keep him from wanting to go back to the *real* love of his life.

"I miss you guys so much. I miss my daughter. I can't wait a whole two weeks for this lockdown to be over, to see her ..."

He's an expert at this waltz. But then I'm always a willing partner. The Dance of a Thousand Deaths.

I know what he's suggesting without him saying it.

"You'd need to do your meetings," I say, throwing down my first bargaining chip.

"Every day," he agrees, "*twice* a day!"

"You *have* to respect my house," I say, because I feel it needs to be said.

"I will."

"I can't have your chaos in the house, Enver. You start and you're out."

"I won't."

"Okay," I say, smiling. "Come now."

And he does, because he loves us, of course, and because this time, *this* time he won't fuck up. He won't.

While I'm waiting for him to walk the three kilometres from his mother's house, I realise that I don't even remember what he looks like. I've read somewhere that trauma can affect the memory. Makes you forget. Could it be that the last year has completely erased my memory to the point that this man whom I've known for 13 years, whose heartbeat I could tap out on a drumhead, whose individual musk I could detect through a forest fire, and whose tongue I could taste out of a million other mouths, has become as much a stranger to my mind's eye as he was the second before I first set eyes on him? If that's the case, then could that be the answer to why I've kept coming back and let him keep coming back all these years? Is it that I've literally forgotten how fucking awful it is? The thought is interrupted by a knock at the front door.

We manage a little less than three days before our crazy starts again. My small house, already cramped with me and Mavis and Zora, becomes positively Lilliputian as soon as Enver arrives with all his baggage, and it doesn't take long for him to become restless. It's like living in a pressure cooker. We're, all of us, struggling with cabin fever, but Enver is catatonic. With him white-knuckling it off the drugs, having to ration his last pack of smokes down to two quick puffs every four hours and in the knowledge that he's just a few streets away from the fix he wants more than anything else on earth, the heat gets turned up to one hundred.

The second he walked back in, the whole atmosphere in the house changed. Like it had been pumped full of noxious gas. Every day the gas just gets thicker and thicker. As much as I know I need to put my gas mask on and cover my eyes, I don't; instead, I just keep breathing in deeper and deeper and blinking through the tears.

One evening after Zora and Mavis are asleep, Enver and I are sitting on the couch watching TV. He looks over at me and pats his lap. I smile and lift my legs onto his. I love it when he rubs my feet. It feels ... religious. I lay my feet on the altar of his knees and pretend to myself that I forgive him – this man who is both Jesus and Judas – for his treachery.

I watch him pouring oil into his hands, ready to anoint me. He curves his thumb against the arch of my foot, pulling it towards the place his heart used to be. When he begins to squeeze, I realise I am holding my breath and I force myself to exhale.

He is back. I try not to wonder how long he will stay this time.

He presses deep into my heels, pushing so hard that it hurts. He could keep pressing and pushing until my bones cracked, one by one, between his long fingers and I wouldn't move. I would lay right here and keep smiling.

He thinks he is making it all better. Better for *him*. Thinks that this is what he needs to do to keep doing what he needs to do. He hasn't looked at me once – we both know he can't – but my feet are in his hands.

When he is done, I am vibrating from my toes to my temples. I want him to vibrate too, so I lean forward and reach for him. Quickly he takes my hand.

But it's too late. I've felt something.

"I love you," he says.

Fuck. I know this game.

"I *love* you," he says again.

"Stand up," I say, knowing he will not.

"I'm hard," he says. "For you." This is desperation.

I can see the outline of something in his nylon tracksuit pants. He knows I felt it.

"Stand. Up."

He stares at me.

"Up!" I can feel a pulse ticking in my jaw.

He stands and a small, brown bottle drops to the floor in the space between our feet. I stand up and walk to the bathroom. I splash cold water on my face. When I come back out, Enver and the bottle are gone.

He reappears the next day, contrite and convincing, and the cycle begins again. In and out, in and out; for weeks he moves back and forth between his mother's house and mine. Can't live with, can't live without. It's excruciating, and yet I become attuned to the unpredictability of it. One day, I become aware of a strange thudding sound. It's incessant. I can't place where it's coming from until, lying in bed at night, with everyone else asleep, I realise it's my own heartbeat.

The anxiety of constantly living on a knife-edge is worse than any depression I've ever known. Where depression feels dim and dark and heavy and laboured, anxiety makes me feel electric and overcharged. Sometimes I'm scared to touch Zora in case a spark flashes straight through me and into her.

Of course, I'm consumed with worry and guilt about how everything is affecting her too. I don't instinctively know what the right thing is to do, for *her*. I'm torn between protecting her *from* him and worrying about the damage it will do to her if I cut him off completely. More concerning is that I don't even know if that's something I'm even *able* to do. Often, I think about just selling up, not telling Enver we're going, and moving to Joburg or even England, believing distance is the only way I'll be able to safeguard Zora from him and from my inability to stop entertaining the madness.

I've been amazed that, despite his inconsistence in her life, she knows exactly who Enver is. Her first word is "Dadda". When he walks through the door, she only has eyes for him. She thrusts her little fat fingers up at him, demanding to be scooped up. She squeals with delight when he covers her with kisses and jabbers away at him every evening when he baths her. All the best parts of Enver are on display in those moments and, when I watch them together, I am reminded of the man I fell in love with. I take mental (and actual) snapshots of these moments so that when she's older and asks about her father and if he was ever around, I will be able to say, "For a while, yes, and he loved you."

"Remember," says my therapist one day when I'm telling him my concerns, "*you* have been her constant. She feels safe and secure because *you* have shown her that consistency. You're doing better that you give yourself credit for." Maybe, maybe not. If I'm doing that great of a job, I think, why can't I stop Enver from disappearing? Living with the constant anticipatory dread of when the "next time" is coming is intolerable.

In the end, when it comes, I can't help but think he couldn't have picked a worse day for it. I've got builders at the house, banging holes in the walls ("to let the air in", apparently), and I'm officially now in the midst of my first bout of serious depression since Zora was born.

I've been to see Dr Dolly and she's managed to convince me, for the first time since I learned I was pregnant, to take something to help. "I don't know why I'm so anxious," I'd stuttered unconvincingly a couple of weeks ago in her reception area, reluctantly reaching out for the prescription and pretending I didn't notice my hand trembling.

In addition to the builders, I've got to go into work to interview some Z-lister who refuses to get up early for a live interview at the weekend – fucking pain-in-the-ass "celebrities" – but I don't want to go. I want to stay at home where I can watch Enver and look out for signs that he's about to flip the table again. It would cause an almighty mess if he did, especially after I've managed to reset everything almost to how it was after the last time, and the times before that. If you look carefully, you can still see the cracks from where everything got broken.

At the meetings, they say that watching won't stop anything bad from happening. *You are powerless over the addict and their using*, they say. *There's nothing you do or don't do that affects why they use. It doesn't work like that*, they say, but it's hard to hear them above the noise of my damn teeth chattering so loudly all the time. Plus, I'm not far enough through the *Living with an Addict: For Dummies* handbook that I'm able to realise when I'm in denial.

I don't know it yet, but it's not actually the relapse itself that I fear the most; it's the deception that comes with it. The dance he makes us go through before he gets caught bang to rights. That's the sucker punch, that's what I can't deal with. His insistence that we go down with the ship too. I *still* haven't learned that I need to secure my life vest first and that, if I just stop trying to save him from himself, there might just be space left on the life raft for all of us.

I've felt it coming again pretty much since he walked back in the last time. At first, it was just a niggling sensation, like a tiny piece of gravel in one's shoe, barely perceptible. But then the red flags start popping up like fucking mushrooms (magic ones, probably) and before long it's like watching a round-the-clock semaphore demonstration in my living room every goddamn day. For the last couple of weeks, it's felt like we're back competing in our own version of *The Hunger Games*, although sometimes it's hard to tell whether it's a death match or simply a fight for our own survival.

He's hovering in the doorway of Zora's room. I'm sitting on the bed, propped up on a unicorn pillow, my laptop purring warmly on my thighs.

"Can I go get my haircut?"

We're at the point where his absence makes me anxious. But, of course, we're at the point where his presence too makes me anxious. We're also at the point where, because of our history, he has to check in with me for *everything*. I think it's building trust and transparency; he says it's co-dependent and controlling. We really are two sick puppies.

I look up from the screen. He's so clever, I think. He knows if I say no, he'll have all the ammo he needs to accuse me of controlling/babying/suffocating/hampering his growth – *so very "unrecovery"*, *SJ*. If I say yes, he's got his out. Whatever caveats I impose on his window of freedom, in the mistaken belief of protecting myself, he'll agree to. Anything, just to get out. To score.

I shift on the bed; the unicorn is stabbing me in the back, my thighs are overheating.

"Sure," I say. The familiar, hot, prickly feeling starts creeping up the back of my neck and I have the sudden urge to shit.

"I would just ask you to remember what we talked about last night. Rebuilding trust. *Transparency*, Enver," I say, sounding like a headmistress.

"Sure," he says. "I'm taking the car – it'll be quicker, okay?"

He doesn't wait for me to answer and in what seems like three seconds he's gone from the doorway to the driver's seat, and I hear the car pulling away and the electric gate setting him free.

Less than three minutes later my phone pings. A picture. The inside of the barbershop. A message: *I'm here, love.*

I reply immediately and a single tick confirms what I've known for a while, but I hit "Dial" just to make sure. The phone doesn't even ring.

"You've reached the mailbox of ... Enver ... please leave a message after the tone."

Motherfucker.

Leaving the builders to their air holes, I half-walk, half-run to the barbershop. It's five minutes away at a pace. I'm bargaining with fuck-knows-who and fuck-knows-what the whole way. What I'll *do*, what I *won't* do, if he can just be there, sitting in the chair, snip, snip, snip, short-back-and-sides, when I get there.

"I'm looking for my husband," I blurt out to a bewildered-looking man blowing hair out of the rusting blades of a pair of clippers.

"For haircut?"

I nod. "My husband, he was here for a haircut, yes?"

"No one here," says the man spinning around, his arms splayed as if to fully demonstrate the emptiness of the salon.

"Thank you," I say. I walk back outside and vomit a mouthful of bile and a stomachful of realisation into the street.

I turn to walk home and see my car coming down the road towards me. The same road where the dealer lives. Initially, I'm puzzled and wonder how my car can be moving without me in the driver's seat. A cloud passes by overhead, dimming the reflection off the glass and I see his face behind the windscreen and remember. He pulls over.

"Out," I demand.

"What's wrong?"

He's inviting me to dance.

"Out!" I repeat.

"Sara-Jayne, what's *wrong?*"

Will we rumba or will we tango?

"*OUT!*" I shriek.

"Just get in the car, please."

A quick two-step and cha-cha-cha.

I know the moves, but this time my feet stay firmly planted. I'm sitting this one out.

"GETOUTOFMYCARYOUMOTHERFUCKER!!"

He gets out, blinking his deceitful dead-black eyes at me. I take my car and my power back, and I drive home.

When I walk through the door, there are three holes in the wall and debris everywhere. I sit down on the kitchen floor and wait for the dust to settle.

25

Round and round we go

He's been gone for close on a month before I realise it's missing. We have, since his last abscondence, the three of us, found ourselves moving back into an Enver-less rhythm of sorts. Without the erratic drumbeat of his constant in and out, we've found a way of existing that's both pragmatic and keeps me on the right side of the thin line of wanting to blow my brains out with a Smith & Wesson. His absence is comforting and catastrophic at the same time. A tragic, gaping relief.

I'm getting ready for work one day when I notice it's gone. I'm scratching in the birchwood cabinet I'd had made for myself as a "push present" when I was expecting Zora. I'm looking for a CD to accompany me the 20 minutes it takes to drive to the studio, notwithstanding the five minutes I may have to spend explaining to an overenthusiastic Officer Du Plessis why I'm flying down the highway in the middle of lockdown.

It feels like a Tupac kinda day, I think to myself, reaching to the back of the cabinet past the Whitney, the Bongo Maffin and the Kelly Khumalo, behind the broken TV remote and the embossed notebook and pen I took from the hotel the last time I was in Joburg. There's the jingle of my keys from Sheila's house, which I still need to return. Evidence of the life I used to live. SJ BC. Before Child. Before Chaos. (Before Covid.)

In addition to looking for something to blast *en route* to work,

I'm also looking-not-looking for the small Bluetooth speaker I'd bought for Mavis when she started working for me five months ago. I realise it's been a while since I've seen it. It had been part of the deal when I hired her. She could live with the no-TV rule, she'd said, but she'd need a radio. She'd never make it through a whole day without uMhlobo Wenene FM. I'd agreed and bought a nifty little Bluetooth speaker with a built-in radio that she'd hated on sight and refused to use, preferring instead to carry out her daily tasks with her headphones plugged into her cracked cell phone, Zora contentedly asleep on her back. The speaker had been chucked into the cabinet with a load of other miscellaneous detritus.

I've stopped looking for the CD and am exclusively focused now on the speaker. I'm tempted to simply reach behind the back panel of the cabinet and pull so that the whole unit comes crashing down and the contents of each compartment are vomited out onto the living-room floor to reveal what I already know. The rage, I think, comes even before the realisation. The absolute fury that he's done it again. The *tweegevriet* boldness of it vibrates in my jaw. I keep looking long after I realise I'm not going to find it.

After work, I make my way home via my usual route until the last kilometre, where I usually go straight, but instead I hang a left and a left again. I don't even allow myself to catch my breath when I pull up outside the police station. Out of the car and in. For too long I've been protecting Enver from the consequences of his behaviour. Through my denial and enabling, I've – albeit inadvertently – been facilitating his drug use. We *all* have. If he's to have any hope at getting clean and staying clean, he's going to have to start feeling some fallout. But, more than that, it's time to start taking back some of *my* power. For *me*. I cannot fix Enver, I cannot stop him from using, but I *can* stop being a victim of it.

"I want to open a case of theft," I tell the officer behind the counter, "against my child's father." I've been dreading this and I'm waiting for the look of judgment. It's the story of my life, carrying shame that doesn't belong to me. But the officer nods kindly and asks, "What was stolen?" The dream, I want to say, but instead I pull a pen out of my bag and start writing:

1 x Bluetooth speaker

1 x pink-and-gold babygro

1 x baby blanket (2 pck)

Cash (unknown, probably thousands)

1 x DVD player

1 x GPS car navigator

1 x iPad

2 x portable phone chargers

1 x hard drive

3 x USB memory sticks

1 x pot of unopened face cream

1 x bottle Sunlight washing-up liquid (unopened)

When I've finished writing, I take a deep breath and slide the page across the desk to the officer. He tells me they'll get on to it when they can, but I can see from the look on his face that it's not a priority. This is Cape Town. Domestic theft isn't top of the priority list. But that's okay. It's not what *they* will do that matters; it's what *I* have done and for whom.

26

The beginning of the end

My legs are swinging several inches above the floor. I'm on the edge of my seat – and higher than I ought to be. I am reminded of the hours I spent on the piano stool as a child, practising my scales and arpeggios, several of my parents' hardback Dickens novels under my bum so I could reach the keys, my feet unmoored, just like now, unable to reach the pedals. Here in the studio, though, I have to be able to reach the pedals because I'm the one in the driving seat. My fingers hover above the "Mic Live" button. Everything comes down to that button. The second I press it, it's show time – lights-camera-action! – and I'm instantly transported into lives that are not my own. If only they knew, I think.

Today's challenge, in the Life and Times of Sara-Jayne, is having to come to terms with the fact that it's unlikely Enver will *ever* come right. Lady H has won, and I'm finally ready to surrender to her, lest our useless battle goes on forever. My heart is broken for Zora and I agonise over how I will explain to her one day that, even though Daddy loved her, he … he … he what? He hated himself more? When she asks me, "Why didn't he love me enough to stop?" I'll say, feeling like a fraud, that it's not as simple as that. How will I make sure that she doesn't take on his abandonment of her as being anything to do with her? I hate that I don't have the answers and I hate myself for letting her down so badly.

For the last few weeks, I've begun trying to focus on the things I need to do if life without Enver is indeed going to be our lot. We can't live in limbo forever, our lives hanging by a thread all the time, precarious and unpredictable. Children need stability. I need stability. It's time for me to rescue us.

I'm still doing the support meetings, which happen online because of the pandemic, and at night, while Zora feeds, I cover us with a blanket, pop my headphones in and listen as people share their stories of hope and despair. I've also joined a couple of single-mom groups on Facebook, although they generally depress the living hell out me. I'm mostly left with two overriding thoughts whenever I scroll through the posts. One, that the answer to the question "How do you do it?" that mothers have been asked for years is "Because we have no damn choice" and, two, men ain't shit.

I last saw Enver two days ago, quite by accident. I was driving with Zora back from her latest paediatric check-up ("growing beautifully") when I spotted him standing on the road doing the "addicts' lurk". I hadn't seen or heard from him since he was caught red-handed and relapsing, so I immediately pulled over and put the window down. A month and a half back on the street and the smack and he looked worse than I've ever seen him. He was back to his uniform of ill-fitting T-shirt, ripped jeans and broken flip-flops. His hair had grown long again, and his beard was unkempt and scraggly. He looked every inch as if he belonged exactly where I found him, but what scared me was that his body looked as if it were incapable of withstanding one more hit. He's going to die soon, I thought.

"What are you doing?" Stupid question, you *know* what he's doing.

"Waiting to score. Where's Zora?" Fuck me. Not even trying to hide it these days. Part of me appreciated his honesty.

"She's here. In the back."

He'd opened the back door and burst into tears at the sight of her gummy smile.

I didn't have it in me to attempt to comfort him. I wasn't even sure who he was crying for. Instead, I'd thought about the last few occasions I'd seen him, how I'd begun to brace myself for each time being the *last* time. The last time we'd ever see him alive. How I'd started to make sure to try to take in every detail of him, for Zora. But it's become more and more difficult. With every bow-out and subsequent encore, the person I once knew as Enver is getting harder and harder to capture. Like trying to take a picture of a ghost.

"How are you?" he'd asked helplessly, both of us knowing that even if I'd said I was about to drive into the ocean with our daughter, he was in no position to do anything about it. For the first time it really struck me that he had lost the power of choice in all of this. He wasn't doing this *to* us, he was doing it to himself, and we were the collateral damage. It wasn't about choosing the drugs over us and, despite all the apparent evidence to the contrary, it wasn't *personal*. It was addiction. I looked at him standing there on the pavement, completely possessed by this thing. One last look. Click-click.

"We'll be fine. Goodbye, Enver," I'd said and driven away.

It's my fortieth birthday, but there's absolutely nothing to celebrate. I'm grateful, though, for the small party my antenatal pals are hosting for me after work and for the kind wishes pouring in from friends and, for the next four hours, listeners. Four hours, I tell myself, you've just got to hold it together for four hours, but I'm struggling to find even the pretence of joy that I've so often before managed to dust off and polish so I can keep up appearances. It's getting harder to pretend that I'm not headed back down the all-too-familiar road signposted "Depression and Despair". It's a place I know well. I've camped out in its rickety, precarious outhouses too many times in my too-long life.

Every day feels like I'm pulling my heavy legs through treacle or tar. Dirty, dark, potentially deadly tar. I think about dying and death a lot. Not mine. I think about crying a lot too, but before I'm even able to form the first of what I'm sure would be an ocean of tears, I remind myself of the futility of it, so I don't bother. Instead, I shake my head madly a couple of times as if performing a bizarre mini-exorcism. "No!" I command. "No!" And, pulling on my worn-out old boots of stoicism, I turn on my heel and follow the signpost marked "Survival". Just for today, I'll survive.

My last guest on the show is South African singer-songwriter Claire Phillips. Claire knows all about surviving. Rape, abuse, suicide attempts, drug addiction. She's overcome it all. Whenever we connect, I feel like I'm talking to a sister and listening to a preacher. Claire is truly one of the good ones. She's on the show to promote her latest single, "Champion". I ask her to explain to the listeners what the track is about.

"When you step into your purpose and your light, you see that the self-destruction is a symptom of what happened. Once you understand that, the only place you can go is up."

Her words strike my solar plexus. Then, as if there's no one else listening, and with no knowledge of the personal strife I'm going through, she says, "I want to say this to you, Sara-Jayne, if *you* are the one in your life that heals, not only do you heal yourself, you heal all the women who came before you and you heal all the kin that is to come from you. And I think that is a beautiful gift to give to your kid."

I can't speak and then, for the first time in almost 20 years of broadcasting, I cry live on air.

Five days after I encountered him on the street and two days after my birthday, he calls. "I'm so sorry, I missed it," he says,

236

as if it were an oversight in his diary and not that he was out on the street jonesing for a hit. He sounds different somehow ... I can't make out what it is.

"Baby, I spoke to Jerome and he gave me a number of a rehab that might be able to offer me a place. I've phoned the guy ... He says he'll let me know when a bed is available. I'm just waiting to hear back."

"That's good," I say. A year ago, I would have jumped for joy. But it's not a year ago.

A few hours later I'm looking down at the cherubic, impossibly beautiful, pink-pyjamaed version of me sleeping comatose on the bed next to me. I idly reach down and stroke my fingers across her soft brow, which, furrowed as it is, makes her look altogether too much like the *other* half of her (and, at one time, the other half of me) who should be occupying the too-big space she inhabits on the mattress. I lean across and whisper in her ear, "It's okay, my love ... Whatever happens, I'll always look after you."

Enver calls early the next day. "The guy called back. He says there's a bed at the rehab. I can go in today."

27

F.I.N.E.

August 2017, Johannesburg

"We can go in. We can go in. *We can go in!*" The authorisation filters up from the bottom of the staircase like Chinese whispers. It's a Tuesday morning, I'm 27 and I've been in rehab for four days.

After years of finding things far less palatable to escape into than the love stories I devoured as a child, I have finally, predictably, in my mid-twenties wiped out and hit a version of rock bottom that requires action.

Three days ago, I arrived from Dubai to embark on what I believe will be a month-long stint "in treatment". Just like in the movies, I'll stay here for 28 days, draw up a family tree, do a collage of my goals, and instantly hate and then tearfully form a lifelong friendship with one of my roommates over our shared shitty lives. I'll find something called a Higher Power, tell some Birkenstocked hippy about how my father never loved me, and then I'll emerge, cured and ready to sashay back into my life, which will be waiting with open arms, full of promises to not be so shitty from now on because, frankly, SJ, you don't deserve it and you've had a bit of a rough deal so far.

From the outside, the rehab looks like a normal house. Inside it's been divvied up to create spaces for up to 20 patients. There are bedrooms up and downstairs (strictly male or female), an office, two individual therapy rooms, a nurses' station, a kitchen/dining room, a rec room and the main Group Room where we gather twice a day to have the emotional shit kicked out of us by a group of no-bullshit addiction therapists.

The Group Room is upstairs, next door to the nurses' station and opposite a cupboard rather ambitiously labelled The Tuck Shop. Since we're not allowed to go into the Group Room without permission, we've gathered on the staircase and are waiting to be given word. It's an arbitrary rule but one that is adhered to with rigid obedience. There's a palpable sense of relief when the signal comes and we are allowed to enter.

The Group Room is neither a large nor a particularly comfortable space. It feels rather like the spare room of a house whose owners have run out of cash and the impetus to decorate, and because of this it's now become the legitimate dumping ground for the things they don't want seen: odd chairs, a broken printer, a box of linen, some CDs without the cases, some cases without the CDs. None of these things are actually *in* the Group Room, though; instead there are three or four stacks of chairs, a pile of yoga mats (for fuck's sake), a flip chart and a CD/cassette player.

We shuffle in ahead of the chief therapist (she actually *is* wearing Birkenstocks), who has been nicknamed the Ice Queen by the other patients and who has the palest skin and bluest lips I've ever seen on a person who is still alive. She looks like a cadaver. She's one of three counsellors at the centre tasked with putting our broken pieces back together again.

She uses her eyes to count the tops of our heads as we file in.

"Fifteen," she announces. "Including me."

Once inside, we sit for a few minutes in agonising silence. The Ice Queen, who is a master at purposefully creating disconcerting and uncomfortable spaces, gives nothing away and blinks indifferently at each of us, slowly and deliberately drawing her paper-thin eyelids over her cold, midnight eyes. "Who would like to start?" she says eventually to the collective relief of the group. And we're off.

"Group", from what I've been able to gather, is all about breaking a bunch of already broken people with the aim of eventually building them up again in a way that ensures they don't have to rely on booze, pills, porn, food, frequent and furious masturbation (public and/or private), punishing exercise, compulsive working, relationships, gambling or *insert drug of choice here* to get through the day. Looking around at my fellow inmates, it seems like an ambitious task.

The worst part is how gladiatorial it appears. I'd been absolutely horrified by my introduction to Group yesterday morning. After an initial and fairly tame "feelings" round, one of the inmates had become the sole focus of the entire session.

Looking not unlike a witch who's down on her luck, Shivon is an older Jewish woman, pushing 70 maybe, with a mass of very obviously dyed jet-black hair and one solitary tooth occupying the space where her top row of teeth should have been. For a full 40 minutes she was shown her asshole, not by the Ice Queen but by the rest of the "recovery community".

It all started when she was asked if she'd had any further thoughts about why her family might have staged an intervention three weeks prior, resulting in her being forcibly thrust into rehab. In response, Shivon fluttered her drugstore eyelashes, pursed her overly lipsticked mouth and let out a little giggle.

"Oh, I don't know, dear," she said, waving her hand dismissively. "I suspect they all just want me in here so they can get their hands on the money."

The Ice Queen raised her eyebrows. "The money?"

"Yes, dear. I've quite a lot of money, you see, left to me by my late husband, and I suspect they, his children, all just want to get their hands on it."

"I see," said the Ice Queen. "Thank you, Shivon."

And, at that, Shivon smiled a decidedly gappy smile at everyone in the room, clearly delighted at having set us all straight, and relieved and ready to give up her position as the centre of attention. But then, just as it seemed we were about to move on, the Ice Queen unfolded a piece of paper she'd been keeping in her lap.

"Do you know what this is, Shivon?" she asked. Shivon shook her head. "This is a letter ... from your stepchildren."

The entire room returned their collective gaze to Shivon, who was now shuffling awkwardly in her seat.

"Wh-what does it say?" she stuttered.

"What do you think it might say?" the Ice Queen smiled.

"Probably lies," spat Shivon, addressing the whole group. "They're *always* telling lies."

"Let's see, shall we?" said the Ice Queen, taking her time unfolding her spectacles, placing them on the end of her narrow nose and shaking out the letter with far more drama than was strictly necessary.

Three chairs down from me, I felt the anger and anxiety radiating off Shivon. While part of me felt terribly sorry for her, another part was desperate to know what was in that letter. It was like watching a car crash in slow motion.

"Shivon," said the Ice Queen, "would *you* like to read this to the group?"

Fuck me. This was next level. I'd never seen anything like it.

Shivon turned green and when she didn't reply, the Ice Queen said, "Or perhaps one of your fellow house members could read it for you?"

At that, Shivon leapt up and practically tore the letter from the Ice Queen's hands.

When she sat back down and began reading, the room fell dead silent. Twice I had to catch myself because my mouth had fallen open.

The letter explained in excruciating detail the *real* reason Shivon was in rehab and it painted an ugly picture, not just of her alcoholism but also of her addiction to cocaine and Xanax, her unbridled gambling addiction (which had seen her losing all of her late husband's considerable fortune and selling off a number of family heirlooms belonging to her stepchildren) and years of compulsive spending. Shivon had racked up eye-watering debts and was on the verge of losing the house *Mr* Shivon had intended to go to his children once he and Shivon were no longer around. At this revelation, we all watched as Shivon's cheeks coloured and a small twitch formed around her lips. We also learned the story behind Shivon's missing teeth. A drunken tumble down several flights of concrete stairs at her local shopping centre (from which she had subsequently been banned) had not only claimed her smile but also almost cost her her life.

When she got to the bottom of the page, her face briefly crumpled at the part where her stepchildren expressed their wish to have absolutely nothing to do with her. For a good three minutes after she finished reading, the entire room remained dead quiet. I was absolutely gobsmacked. Shivon was a *proper* addict. She was fucked.

"So sex, drugs and rock 'n' roll, hey, Shivon?" The Ice Queen broke the unbearable silence. "Right, who'd like share back to Shivon on their observations?"

And then, for the next half an hour, the group went in for the kill. No holds barred. "Denial is not a river in Egypt", "completely manipulated the people who cared for you", "secrets keep you sick", "put your addiction before everything", "telling lies but you're the only one who believes them", "nearly died, so when is enough enough?", "dishonest, manipulative and selfish", "liar who only thinks of herself" – the observations (and accusations) came thick and fast.

Shivon was crucified by everyone in the group; it was brutal and I was horrified. If this was rehab, I'd sooner take my chances as a bulimic, co-dependent drunk. I was nowhere near as bad as Shivon, so I thought, but I was terrified that when my turn came to be in the hot seat, as it clearly would, I would receive a similarly savage dressing-down.

At one point, Shivon tried (unsuccessfully) to defend herself, but she was immediately shot down by Duran, a teenaged crackhead already on his fourth sojourn in treatment. "You can't bullshit a bullshitter, Shivon," he shrugged.

"But, Duran, my dear, *all* of you, I'm telling the truth!" she pleaded.

"Oh, Shivon!" he barked back at her. "Stop lying through your tooth." At that, even the Ice Queen struggled to keep a straight face.

Three days prior, when I'd arrived at the centre, I'd been presented with an A4 notebook and pen and told that I would need to start writing down my life story. It was something each patient was required to do, they said. I assumed it would be given to my therapist so he or she (*she*, as it turned out, as I'd been assigned to the Ice Queen) could work out the best way to cure me and so, immediately the following morning, with a full pack of Marlboros and a mainline of coffee, I diligently began writing and didn't stop until midnight. As instructed, I slid the entire 14 pages under the door of the counsellor's office before turning in for the night.

Now, sitting in Group, listening to everyone checking in, I can see the Ice Queen reaching into the folder she carries with her and pulling out a substantial wad of papers. Which poor bastard's in the dock today, I wonder as she smooths the pages along her lap with her hand.

When everyone has finished sharing "what's going on for them", the Ice Queen pulls her face into one of her deadly, cool-as-fucking-ice smiles and says, "Sara-Jayne."

I look around, waiting for the other Sara-Jayne to identify herself.

"You. Sara-Jayne," says the Ice Queen, pointing at me with her glasses. "You've been here for five days now. I think we'd all like to get to know you better." The words are congenial enough, but the tone is arctic. I say nothing because I'm not really sure how to respond. I needn't worry because, clearly, this is not Ice Queen's first rodeo.

"Your life story," she says patting the papers on her lap. "Are you ready?"

Ready for what? She's not seriously expecting me to relay every miserable detail of my life to a bunch of crazies I've known for less than a week, surely? Except that she is. She's already passing around the circle my life on paper; my wounds and sores, my shame and self-doubt being fingered by the hands of strangers. I don't like this type of spotlight. This type of attention.

There's no time to object and I sense it would be pointless anyway. Taking my life story in my hands, I start reading: *"I've always known there was something wrong with me ..."*

I *always* felt there was something wrong with me. Fundamentally. I always felt that I was *different*, not like other people. Not just because I was the wrong colour – although being one of only two real-life, not-on-TV black people I knew throughout my entire whitewashed upbringing was unlikely to make me feel an overwhelming sense of belonging – but more than that. I felt different on the *inside* as well as the outside.

I always thought that I cried too easily and laughed too loudly. Everything I felt was so ... *big*. Big happy, big sad, big love, big mad. My feelings were always so overwhelming, like they might at any moment topple me from the high balance beam of life and send me crashing to the hard floor beneath, a jumbled mass of broken bones.

I always had the sense that I was playing catch-up. Like I'd missed a crucial lesson in the Life Skills for Dummies curriculum where you were taught how to navigate both the banal and bewildering aspects of life. Everyone else seemed to get it, whereas I was always floundering, treading water in a tricky, unpredictable sea, my legs frantically pedalling below the surface in anxious anticipation of the next wave that might come crashing down on my head. The vast majority of my 27 years seemed to have been spent coughing saltwater out of my lungs and struggling to keep my head above water.

Most of all, though, I just never felt good enough. But maybe that's just what happens when you're given away as a baby and grow up in a place that sounds like an apology.

As for most addicts, my addictions started innocently enough. Born as coping mechanisms during childhood to help me deal with the discomfort I felt at being me. A way to emotionally self-regulate amid the dysfunction around me. They were behaviours in which I sought refuge as I attempted to exert control over something, *anything*, because so much of what was happening in my world seemed so uncontainable. Even before things got really bad, it was textbook self-medication.

The truth about addiction is that anything can become a gateway drug if the underlying wound isn't properly treated. The escape provided by the harmless but compulsive reading when I was a small child was the same that I sought later in bingeing, purging and starving myself of food. It was the same reason I cut myself with knives and razors and burned myself with lit cigarettes. And it was why, by the time I was in my twenties, I began to seek oblivion in booze and pills. It's also why so often when people quit one addiction, they pick up another almost immediately in its place.

But, like all addictions, the benefits that mine once promised to deliver had a shelf life. They weren't prepared to keep shoring me up for free. And after a while they began to demand payment for services rendered, and the currency they operated in was high: health, wealth, self-worth and ultimately sanity. That's the fucked-up thing about addiction, that the very thing that once saved us can become the thing that nearly kills us. It's like tumbling into a raging river and clinging to a log to keep afloat, but then not letting go of the damn log once the water's calm and you can swim safely to shore. Where I'd given each of my crutches an inch, they had, in the absence of ever being replaced with something healthier, taken a mile.

Eventually, I reach the final paragraph of my life story. When I'm done, there is the inevitable silence from the group. Reading everything out loud has shone a light on parts of my life I have long sought to keep in the dark, hidden from view. I feel prickly raw but also unburdened. Like I'm now wearing my insides on my outside, but I'm lighter.

"How are you feeling, Sara-Jayne?" says the Ice Queen after the requisite millennia of silence have passed.

Instinctively, because it's been what I've been saying for years, I say, "Fine."

As if directed by some invisible cue, the entire room choruses back to me: "Fine is not a feeling."

"*Really*," I say. "I'm fine."

"We're all fine in here – right, guys?" pipes up Duran. "F.I.N.E." He spells it out. "Fucked up, insecure, neurotic and emotional!" Everyone chuckles and nods in knowing agreement.

The Ice Queen ignores the temporary hubbub and says, "How long do you plan to keep lying to yourself, Sara-Jayne?" I'm not used to this type of direct communication. It's not something I've ever been taught, and I flush hot, red from my earlobes to the soles of my feet.

"I-I-I-I'm not lying," I stutter.

"Okay, well, let's see what everyone else thinks, shall we?

Who'd like to give Sara-Jayne some feedback?" Several eager hands shoot up.

Without sugarcoating their words or their delivery, my fellow addicts give it to me straight. They say that my *real* problem, the thing that has brought me to this point, is not any particular substance or behaviour. It's not food – either the gluttonous consumption or the wilful and exhausting rejection of – and neither is it booze. "It's not how much you drink, Sara-Jayne, it's *why* you drink!" It isn't pills, although "normal people don't take 15 codeine for breakfast, Sara-Jayne". Nor is it the succession of disastrous relationships with equally disastrous men I've lost myself to over the years. "Do you realise you've only ever dated men who are emotionally unavailable?" It's none of those things, apparently. I'm confused. If too much food, booze, pills and thrills aren't my problem, why the hell am I in rehab? As if reading my thoughts, the Ice Queen chimes in.

"Our problem as addicts," she says, "is our inability to deal with life on life's terms." She uses those exact words, as if Life is a real person with a living, breathing will. An entity with the ability to create "terms".

"Bullshit!" screams my inside voice. "I'm doing a great job at life – it's the people, places and things *in* my life that are always fucking me over." It's all I can do not to react. The last thing I want to do is lose it like Shivon the other day. But it's quite the task. So, too, is trying to hide my fury that I'm wasting a significant portion of my future inheritance paying for this psycho-babble. The Ice Queen doesn't come cheap.

"My life really isn't that bad," I mumble defensively. Although, judging by the way Ice Queen is looking straight at me, it's clear she knows not only that she is hitting the nail right on my knucklehead, but also that I'm more than getting my money's worth. I force myself to meet her eyes and do my best to stare back at her with the same cool self-assuredness she is radiating. I last about three seconds before I pull my eyes away. Game, set and match to the professional in the Jesus-creepers.

Group is dismissed, but on our way out, the Ice Queen pulls me aside.

"Just because you carry something well doesn't mean it isn't heavy. Maybe just sit with that for a while, see what comes up for you."

Downstairs, while everyone heads to the dining room for lunch, I go outside to chain-smoke my way through a box of Marlboros and think about why I said I was fine, when I'm clearly not. Maybe I *am* a liar?

I've often thought that, had I not ended up falling into a career in journalism, and if I hadn't suffered from a constant, crippling fear of rejection, I'd have managed to carve out a not unlucrative career as an actress. Not Oscar-worthy or award-winning perhaps, but certainly bread-on-the-table, bit-part performances in soap operas or a six-part detective series here or there.

In reality, the likelihood of regular knock-backs from steely-faced casting directors meant that I never seriously considered acting as a career beyond a pipe dream, but I always loved it. It dawns on me that playing a role and putting on a show is something I learned to do, subconsciously, when I was a child, when I felt the need to make things okay.

Some of my earliest and fondest memories are of playing make-believe, escaping to worlds created in my own vivid child's consciousness. That was way before part of me was seduced by the hidden and the secretive and sought the escapism provided by far more harmful pursuits. It was while I still believed that life was playgrounds and candy floss. I'd spend hours dreaming up pretend lives and characters whose shoes and souls I could slip into. Back before I felt compelled to squeeze the atoms of myself into stifling nooks and unseen crannies where shame and silence stroke your hair and hum melodies into your ear so that you lie down with them without a fight and, without even realising it, allow yourself to be comforted by your tricky new bedfellows.

The Ice Queen's words come back to me as I draw deeply on cigarette after cigarette. "Just because you carry something well doesn't mean it isn't heavy." I come to see that I spent an awful lot of my childhood and adolescence convincing people that I was okay. Maybe all it means is that I'm a really good liar or that my poker face is second to none, but then maybe it's not that at all. Maybe it wasn't that I was that good an actress, but rather that those who were supposed to be paying attention weren't.

In the end, it had become clear that 28 days would never cut it for me and, in fact, it was several long, hard months before I eventually left treatment. Clean, sober and no longer under any illusion that I was "fine". That's what going to rehab will do to you. It'll make you realise that you're way more screwed up than you on your own could ever have imagined. You check in thinking you're there to deal with one thing and you leave with an entire treasure trove of unearthed childhood trauma, co-addictions and personality disorders. In fact, if you leave with only what you came in with, you really weren't trying hard enough.

Going to rehab is kind of like going to Woolies. You pop in for a pint of milk and some loo roll and you emerge 40 minutes later weighed down with two punnets of hand-picked raspberries, some organic goat's milk yoghurt, something called a date ball and a fucking corn-fed rotisserie chicken. An entire shopping basket of shit you never bargained (or budgeted) for. Just like rehab.

28

A new creation

When my brother died in 2001, the few belongings discovered next to his body by the police were returned to my mother in a big, black plastic bag. I remember sitting on her dining-room floor sorting through his life in objects, trying to make sense of everything. There were a couple of cigarette lighters, an empty weed bankie and a packet of Rizlas with the top flap torn off (to make a roach for his joints), an ID tag and a set of keys – all things I'd been able to reconcile with the person I'd known when his heart still pumped in his chest.

There had also been a diary and, at that, I had been surprised. The Adam I knew, or thought I knew, didn't keep a diary? Certainly, in the latter years of his too-short life I had been unable to imagine that his mind ever ventured further than where his next drink or hit was coming from. On the last few occasions which I'd seen my brother, I had only been able to catch glimpses of the person I remembered from my early childhood. Addiction had by then, it seemed to me, all but taken over and shrunk his life to the very smallest possibility of living.

With the diary in my hands, I sat on the floor pondering whether it would be an intrusion to read it, while at the same time desperate in my grief to connect one more time with my big brother. In the end, I reasoned that the dead were not likely to be as concerned with privacy as they would have been in life.

Within those pages I discovered that, even though it *felt* as if Adam was close to being completely erased, the sensitive, sweet, introspective, loving brother I had once known *was* actually still in there. Every day he wrote a list of things he was grateful for and, heartbreakingly, every Sunday he would write: "Tomorrow I am going to stop drinking." The entries in his diary were a tragic reminder to me that Adam had never stopped being Adam. In spite of it all, my brother was so much more than just "a drunk". So much more than his pain. So much more than the things he did to stop hurting.

No single one of us is only *one* thing.

It's a little over 12 months since I dropped Enver off at rehab. For the first month we hadn't been allowed any contact at all. It had been a blessed relief. Knowing that he was safe but also that I *couldn't* speak to him gave me some peace of mind, the kind for which I'd have sold my soul to the devil over the previous 18 months.

As I drove away, the relief was the only thing I could really feel grateful for. This would be Enver's fifth, sixth, maybe seventh time in rehab. What would make this time any different from all the times before, or was it just a place he could be that would keep him safe from himself and off the streets for a while? I knew from my own experience that rehab was no guarantee of anything. The real journey begins *after* you walk out of treatment and into real life. Sobriety, in that sense, is a decision. Using is an option that is either on the table or off. If it is off, then everything has to come second to recovery. My once-held steadfast belief that Enver could do anything he put his mind to had long evaporated into the same thin air in which his empty promises resided. I had absolutely no idea whether Enver was capable of or even interested in the commitment, introspection or honesty that long-term recovery demanded.

I was down to my last dime of hope, and my pockets were completely empty as far as faith was concerned.

While Enver was out of sight and, to a degree, out of mind, I had some work to do of my own. I needed to right things with his mother, for Zora's sake. She was almost one and had seen her grandmother only two or three times. None of this mess was her fault and, regardless of Enver's presence in her life, she had a right to know his side of her family. I knew it wouldn't be easy, and that I would have to put my own feelings aside. I also knew that I would have to be the one to initiate any peace agreement between us. I sent his mother a message asking if I could visit her at home.

It was difficult. I was still *very* angry and hurt, but remembering why and who I was doing it for acted as a motivation to do what, deep down, I believed was right. My own recovery programme demanded that I keep my side of the street clean and make amends. I apologised for the way I'd behaved during the pregnancy, the litany of vitriolic messages I'd sent, and the furious outburst at her house. I told her that I would like her to be a part of Zora's life. She said she was sorry for the way things had worked out and slowly she began to become a familiar and regular presence in Zora's life.

My own mother and I had also, tentatively, been able to forge a path away from the painful past and reach safer, softer ground. She seemed delighted by her only grandchild and, even though, thanks to Covid, theirs had become a relationship that existed via the digital ether, Zora loved her regular video calls with Granny and, for the most part, I managed to keep my expectations in check.

A month after he'd gone in, we were allowed to visit Enver at the rehab. Not knowing what I'd find when we got there, I was in two minds on whether to take Zora along, but Mavis convinced me. "Remind him what he's fighting for," she said, dressing Zora in her cutest outfit and coaxing her hair into two little bunches. I didn't say so, but part of me wondered whether he was even still there. It wouldn't be the first treatment centre he'd skipped out on in his rehab career. What if all the time I thought he was secure within its walls he was back out on the street? It's always the not knowing.

I pulled up outside the centre. Behind the gate, a tall, heavy-set man with a shaved head was hanging out what looked to be bedsheets on a makeshift washing line. From behind he looked like a rugby prop. Across his broad back, on his T-shirt, were the words, "This is what recovery looks like." I switched off the engine and the man turned around.

It took me more than a moment to realise it was Enver. He must have put on at least 10 kilos. In addition to the T-shirt, he was wearing a pair of blue jeans and dark grey sneakers. Everything fit him perfectly. It had been so long since I'd seen him looking healthy that I struggled to reconcile the person in front of me with the smack-ravaged Enver of the past couple of years. I even scanned his arms for his telltale tattoos to make sure it was really him. I climbed out of the car and for a second we stood, just staring at one another on either side of the tall metal gate.

"You're fat!" I managed eventually and he laughed. Then he asked me how *I* was, and I felt like I might cry, so I lifted Zora out of her car seat and said in a too-chirpy voice, "Look who it is!" For a second, she looked puzzled; for the last month she'd only seen Enver in pictures and videos on my phone. I braced myself, ready for her little face to crumple, but instead she giggled, reached up and grabbed Enver's nose. "Dadda!"

I couldn't stop staring at him. A month earlier I had all but given up hope that I'd ever again see the Enver I had fallen in love with. His behaviour had been so demonic at the height of his using that I struggled to see him as anything but the devil.

But now, here he was. The *real* Enver. Standing in front of me, like he'd returned from the dead.

"You look so … different."

He smiled. "I've been eating, and gymming every night before the meetings or group. And someone at the church blessed me with some new threads," he said bashfully, brushing nonexistent fluff from his jeans.

"You look really good," I said, "but it's not the weight or the clothes. I don't even know how to describe it. You just look … different. At peace."

"I am."

And so we visited every weekend and, after a couple of months, Enver was allowed to leave the centre for entire weekends, returning on a Sunday evening. We'd spend our two days going for outings to the beach, taking long drives or relaxing at home, just the three of us. Like a *normal* family. The ordinariness of it was exquisite. Often Enver would cook, making sure there was a stocked freezer for the week ahead and that the house was clean and the washing done. He seemed anxious to do his part, knowing that for so long I'd shouldered the burden alone. I took this to be his penance and had no qualms about letting him do it.

One day I decided it might be fun to visit our friend, Mel. Things had changed so much since that awful time in the hospital after Zora was born and, as someone I'd often turned to for support during the worst of Enver's using, I wanted her to see just how well he was doing. We were already on the road when I called her.

"Hi! We were thinking of coming through to see you," I said brightly.

There was a long pause.

"Darling, I'm sorry, but Enver is not welcome in our house. The fact is, we can't trust him – we don't know what he might steal. He can come when he's a year clean."

I pressed the phone closer to my ear in the hope Enver couldn't hear what was being said, but he seemed preoccupied, chatting away to Zora.

"I get it," I said. And I did. This was bound to happen. Addiction has consequences. I hung up and slipped my phone back into my bag.

"So, what's happening?" asked Enver, still pulling faces at a grinning Z in the back seat. "What did Mel say?" He was also grinning.

"You're not going to like this," I warned. "But she says you're not welcome at the house." I don't know what I expected his reaction to be. A few months before, something like that would have set him off.

I saw a muscle in his cheek twitch, but then he smiled. "Okay," he said, "But next time you talk to her, tell her I'll see her on my one-year sober birthday – and I'll cook for all of us!"

I smiled and nodded, but Mel's comment had struck a nerve. A stark reminder of the extent of the damage caused by Enver's using. I had been so seduced by the "new" Enver and his transformation that I was focusing only on the present and not the wreckage of the past. The relief that we seemed finally free of the chaos outshone what had come before and the arduous journey that lay ahead. Enver and I were enjoying our own honeymoon period and he was floating along on his pink cloud – the euphoria experienced by addicts in early recovery – and for a while the past was able to fade into memory.

It did not, however, take long to catch up to the present and we were soon brought back down to earth with an almighty crash. As the one-day-at-a-times became weeks at a time, reality began to kick in in a way neither Enver nor I were prepared for.

In the early days of attending the family-of-addicts' support meetings, I would often hear members talk about how important it was to "prepare for recovery" – a notion I wasn't quite sure

I understood. As far as I was concerned, my problems were in the here and now and started and stopped with Enver's drug addiction. If only *he* would stop using, then everything else would be okay, surely? And I believed the meetings would teach me *how* to get him to stop. As long as I created an environment that would make him want to stop, he would. I truly believed I could fix him, and not in an arrogant way; I thought that if I loved him enough, made him feel good about himself, supported him, he wouldn't *need* to use. But my theory left absolutely no room for Enver's own unhealed traumas, his own choices or the unrelenting *mental* obsession that came with addiction. I also couldn't see that my co-dependency provided the perfect home for his using – in a way, they needed one another to survive.

Nearly 13 years in recovery myself, I'd forgotten everything I knew about addiction. Every day, I dusted off my halo of self-righteousness, put on my rose-tinted glasses and slid my feet into my wishful-thinking boots. I fastened a cloak of denial around my shoulders, fixed my know-it-all badge to my lapel and climbed aboard the If-he'd-just-do-what-I-say Express Train, clutching my ticket to the City of Unrealistic Expectations.

I remember watching an interview with the American actress and recovering addict Jane Fonda years and years ago. "Emotionally healthy people don't get into relationships with drug addicts," she said. And she was right. Every year I'd chalk up another recovery chip handed out at AA and NA meetings for years clean and sober, but *my* biggest sickness, the one that could kill me as easily as all the others, was still alive and kicking.

Before anything else, I was a love addict. Before the food, the booze, the pills, it was *love* that I craved above all else. Love (or the fantasy of it) I would abandon myself for time and again. Love that I thought would fix me and fill the "hole in my soul". Just as Paul Sunderland described in that lecture hall

256

in London, the "hunger for attachment", the primal wound, caused at the very beginning of my life by the abandonment of the *one* person who was meant to stick around. That was the source of my desperation for love and, over the years, the wound had festered deeper and deeper with every loss of love, every abandonment, every time I went looking for love in all the wrong places, until eventually in Enver I saw a place where I could try to rewrite history.

In the early months of his sobriety, because I believed it was Enver who had broken us, I also believed that it was up to him to fix us, and *my* contribution was to scrutinise his recovery. As long as he stayed clean, *that* was all that mattered, so I focused my attention on him and the things he was (or, I felt, *wasn't*) doing to make sure that the chaos of active addiction was never allowed to return to our lives. It never dawned on me that what I really ought to be doing was securing my *own* oxygen mask. I was putting all my eggs in one basket and asking someone with a broken arm to carry it without as much as cracking a single shell.

The absolute terror that Enver would relapse yet again made me hold on even tighter, policing his recovery efforts, thinking my enabling was helping, trying desperately to control everything because, after all, no one would expect me to just sit back and watch the wheels fall off while there was so much at risk, would they?

What I didn't realise, though, was that my "helping" was actually *hindering* and getting in the way of my own healing. I didn't realise that my need to patch everything together and slap a big, shiny red bow on it had nothing to do with Enver and everything to do with my own need to be needed and my absolute fear of being abandoned. I didn't realise that, despite what I told myself, I *wasn't* in control and nothing *I* did would keep Enver clean or stop him from using. I didn't realise he was on his own journey. I didn't realise I was as sick as he was. I didn't realise that *my* co-dependency fed off all this shit. I just didn't realise. And the day I *did* eventually realise, I was left with a decision to make. But for months it felt as if we were taking one step forward and two steps back.

We're told in recovery that the goal is "progress, not perfection", but my anxiety demanded perfection. There were times when we'd catch glimpses of the old Enver, when his addict behaviour crept back in, and it was like we were instantly catapulted back into the past. I'd physically *feel* the terror moving through my body. There wasn't much he did that didn't trigger me. If he was too happy, or too sad, too affectionate, too distant. For months, I made him piss and shit with the bathroom door open so I could be sure he wasn't up to anything. Once, when Zora was sick, I threw out an entire bottle of her medicine because I was terrified he might be using it to hide methadone. I couldn't trust *anything* he said or did. I lived in a state of permanent hyper-vigilance, always waiting, looking for signs that he was going to upend the table again, waiting for the rug to be pulled out from under me. I lived in constant fear that we were one wrong move (by either of us) away from him relapsing and dragging us back down into hell with him.

We began to see a family counsellor, and in therapy we were forced to interrogate the realities of our relationship. Who we were when we met and whether, as two broken souls, we were even capable of the love we so freely professed for one another. I had to ask myself the question I'd been avoiding for years. What if there was no "meant to be"? What if, in fact, it was never even love at all but rather two desperate and disparate damaged souls who collided on their journey to the possibility of healing and took a major detour?

We were forced, too, to examine the dysfunction of our respective childhoods and the abuse and sickness within our own families. Addiction *is* a family disease. It might be that one person is using, but the *whole* family (if they weren't already) becomes sick. Therapy allowed Enver and me to see the entirely messed-up template we both had for relationships and what we had come to believe love should look like. We had always loved hard, but we fought and fucked dirty, believing that without the rocketing highs and crashing lows, the "No, fuck *YOU*s!" and the "Oh, yes, fuck *ME*s!", we weren't entitled to call it love.

I began to see that a big part of my desperation to be with Enver wasn't rooted in my love for *him* but in my own need to be loved. And even though there were glimmers now of the Enver I had been so drawn to all those years ago – a good man with a *good, kind* heart – I was fighting to be with a person, a new creation, that neither he nor I really knew yet.

The revelations that came through our therapy sessions were difficult and painful, but gradually, over the months, life stopped existing on a knife-edge. My shoulders dropped and I stopped bracing myself for the next catastrophe. But it also dawned on me that I'd been in survival mode since my pregnancy, like a cat on a hot tin roof. For almost two years there had been no room to breathe, to process or to heal. There had only been Enver and his using, me and my trauma, and the four of us lurching from one crisis to the next.

The realisation of everything coincides with the arrival of an anger so potent that it frightens me. It's been there all along, of course, simmering just under the surface, like lava, waiting for an opportunity to erupt. I can feel that an explosion is imminent and that it has the power to destroy everything. I'm also aware of a voice I heard a long time ago telling me, "You cannot heal in the same place where you got sick."

"I can't do this," I tell Enver one day. "We should be focusing on being the best parents we can be to Zora, but all this other stuff is getting in the way. I'm so angry I can't see straight and if I don't get a handle on it, it's going to jeopardise everything."

Once upon a time, the anger served a purpose. It gave me the fire I needed to survive. Now it was redundant but still capable of doing irreparable damage to the very thing I was trying to salvage. I know I don't need it any more, but I can't seem to shake it off. I'm forced to accept that I cannot get rid of the *anger* without treating the wound from which it comes.

"Enver, we're not giving ourselves a fighting chance because we're trying to revive something that died a long time ago. I want you to be healthy and happy. I want *me* to be healthy and happy."

And so, we take "us" off the table and make a commitment to focus on our individual journeys of healing. It is excruciating and terrifying and the only possible thing left to do.

29

SJ, heal thyself

It used to be that my favourite time of day was actually night. There was something about the silence and the stillness that made me feel as if I were the only person in the world and that the darkness would keep my secrets. I'm not entirely sure when that changed, but these days I prefer the mornings. Early. Still quiet, but nothing hidden. I love the moment when the sun is coming up and everything under it, including me, is brought into the light.

We are walking in line. Ten of us. Women. Black. Survivors. Ten pairs of footprints pressed into the sand. The weight of our grief draped heavy but unseen across our shoulders. We are silent, rendered so by the ocean's command that we listen as it speaks. We walk until the sun signals for us to be still. We stand at the water's edge and remove our clothes. We are here to stand in our pain. We are here to hold and be held. We are here to heal.

Each one of us steps forward in turn, bringing ourselves and our souls to the ocean in ceremony. Strangers, but also sisters. Mothers, daughters. We stand in silence and, one by one, step forward and speak our pain to the water. Breathing deeply, I bear witness to two, three, four women delivering themselves *to* themselves and *from* themselves. Then a hand, outstretched, beckons me forward. I move to where the sea meets the sand and feel hands on either side of me holding mine.

I close my eyes. A shock of cold. Water is being poured onto me, a baptism.

"It is time to release that which no longer serves you."

The water runs over my head, down over my eyelids, my lips, my breasts, my belly.

"Let go and let it go."

I start to sob. Loud and raw, from the place inside me that only the divine knows. The waves pull me deeper into the ocean. Hands move to my shoulders and around my waist, steadying me, and waves of my own roll and crash. I take a deep breath and allow myself to be pulled under. For a time, I belong to the water, I *am* the water.

When I come back up, mother arms hold me and sister hands wipe my eyes and help me find my centre on the sand again. In silence, we walk back the way we have come. Ten of us. Women. Black. Warriors. Creating fresh new footprints alongside the impressions of the past.

It is nearly 15 years since I sat in a cold lecture hall in a library in South-West London listening, for the first time, to someone speaking about my life, my *truth,* in a way that felt familiar, validating and vital. Paul Sunderland's explanation of how unresolved trauma would go on to manifest in the lives of people like me through addiction and co-dependency was, even if I didn't know it at the time, one of the most profound moments of my life.

For a long time, though, it was unthinkable that I would revisit the past and the root of all that suffering because I wasn't sure I'd survive it a second time, and even if I did, what if I *couldn't* move past it? But, in avoiding it, all that happened was that I subconsciously kept putting myself in situations in which I'd be triggered. I ended up constantly reliving the thing I most wanted to forget. Time, in fact, does not heal all wounds and trauma is cumulative. It *doesn't* resolve itself on its own; it is literally stored in the body, and the body keeps score.

The realisation that the fear of facing my trauma head on was destroying the very thing I had been searching for my whole life was a turning point for me. I could no longer circumvent the trauma, and until I made a commitment to be present in the pain and heal the wounds of the past, I was, as they say, condemned to repeat it. So I started doing the work, breaking the cycle. For me. For *Zora* and for the generations who would come after us.

I was well into my twenties and my heart more than a little bruised before I realised that the books, the soap operas, the rom-coms and the Teddy Pendergrass lyrics I'd relied on to tell me what love should look and feel like might have sold my innocent young heart a lie. But by then the damage had long been done. I was desperate and determined. A deadly combination in the name of love.

It's taken a good portion of my 41 years to surrender to the fact that, in all likelihood, the type of love I've been so desperately trying to fall into since I first set eyes on young Simon Shakespeare *doesn't* actually exist and, even if it does, I don't want it any more. The type of love I want today starts with me; it has to. What I'm learning as I heal is that anything, any*one* that comes in the name of love must come to complement, not complete me. People can never be who we want them to be, just because we want them to be. They can only be who they are, and only they have the power to change themselves. No one exists to fix another person; we cannot be the elixir that heals someone else's wounds. It is up to us to heal our *own* hurts, even when we may not have caused them. If we do not, we risk becoming hurt people who hurt people.

There was something else Paul Sunderland said that day in London that also stuck with me. Referencing a study on attachment by the University of California, Berkley, in the mid-eighties, he said that the emotional stability of a child was 75 per cent dependent on the parent, *particularly* the mother, being able to *know* herself, meaning being able to tell an emotionally coherent story about herself. If the mother can do that, then the child has a very good chance of being well balanced.

It's a notion that has been somewhat bastardised by the meme generation and often appears modified and oversimplified as the quote "*When you can tell your story without crying, you know you have healed*", but the premise is the same.

Of course, healing is not linear, just as recovery is not a destination. But my commitment to both is the greatest gift I can give to myself, and I owe it to my children. To *tell* my story is to heal. So here it is. It's not perfect, but it's a start.

Epilogue

A lot can happen in a year. That's what I'm thinking as I attempt to corral five enormous rose-gold balloons into the back seat of my car. A maverick cerise 2 won't fall in line and keeps threatening to make a break for freedom. I struggle for a minute, frustrated, but then see the futility in it and stop fighting. Eventually the 2 floats down and is persuaded, by a gentle gust of wind, to find itself a home in Zora's car seat. Sometimes things need to find their own way in their own time; they can't be forced.

I drive home, marvelling that the little creature who just yesterday, it seems, existed as a heartburn-inducing watermelon resting on my pelvic bone is today turning a whole two years old. At 24 months, Zora is an exact and delightful mix of her father and me. In looks and temperament. The best of us both. Like him, she is kindly and shy at times. She's an observer, a watcher of people and a very good judge of character. Like me, she is a lover of books and melodies. Like us both, she is deeply sensitive and fiercely determined. She has Enver's eyes, my nose and her late rakgolo-khuhku's gap-toothed smile. Best of all, she has an enormous heart. She is a child who loves and knows she is loved.

Pulling up, I can already hear shrieks of laughter from inside the house. I push open the gate, carrying the wayward balloons in one hand and a bag of gifts (hidden in my car for the last week for safekeeping) in the other. Zora, in pyjamas and wellies, gallops into the garden and hurls herself at me in delight.

"Mama! Mama!" She sees the balloons and squeals. "'Loons! 'Loons!"

"Hello." Enver is standing on my patio smiling. "How was work?"

I smile back. "It was good, thanks."

Zora has taken off with the balloons and is high-tailing it around the garden.

"Ma, look – 'loons! 'loons!" Excitedly, she shows them off to her grandmother who is standing in the doorway laughing and taking pictures on her phone. "Ma hold, Ma hold!" demands Zora, thrusting one of the balloons at Enver's mother, and of course, Ma holds. We coax Zora indoors and convince her to sit down long enough to get *my* mother on a WhatsApp call. From 9 000 kilometres away, she is beamed into my living room to watch Zora open her presents. She unwraps a beautiful set of wooden musical instruments from my mum.

"What do you say, Zora?" prods Enver.

"Thankoo, Ganny!" says Zora, jangling a tambourine at the phone. "Thankoo! Thankoo! Thankoo!"

Thank you, indeed.

Thanks to:

Z-J, Mum, Dad and my siblings Thabo, Thabiso and Mokgadi. Ben (and Joao ☺), Holly Gibson, Gina King, Susan Rabinowitz, Martina Dahlmanns and family, Thoko Madonko, Julie Mentor, Youandi Gilian, Gabbi Theys, Jess Randall, Louise Edwards, Melody Schneider, Natasha Schermbrucker, Jody, Amy, Jess and Rebecca, Mish Thomas, Claire Phillips. My *CapeTalk* listeners. My recovery family "in the rooms". Dot, Alex, Claudia and Paul Sunderland. EN.

Thanks also to NB Publishers, Sean Fraser and Riaan Wolmarans. And *huge* thanks to Melinda Ferguson Books, and Melinda Ferguson for your unwavering belief in me. (*"Dear Ms Ferguson, I'd like to write a book ..."* Hahaha!)

And to the countless other kind souls who have provided support, love, encouragement and zero drama – thank you.